D1499639

# Pope Pius XII

*"Supreme Doctor,
Light of Holy Mother Church,
Lover of the Divine Law."
("Doctor Optimus,
Ecclesiae Sanctae Lumen,
Divinae Legis Amator.")*
**John XXIII**

by

Margherita Marchione

ÀNCORA EDITRICE
Via G.B. Niccolini, 8 - 20154 Milan
Italy

N.A. 4348 – ISBN 88-514-0156-X
Printed in Italy by ÀNCORA ARTI GRAFICHE, Milan

*To His Holiness Pope John Paul II,*
*who strengthened the Church in a period of turmoil,*
*reached out to all other religions,*
*and became the world's leading moral voice*
*for life, tolerance, charity and peace.*
*In this he continues and expands*
*the work of charity and love of Pope Pius XII.*
*The link between these two outstanding pontiffs*
*becomes more apparent the more one studies their lives.*

3

*Acknowledgments: The author is grateful to Ralph M. Cestone for providing the finances to publish this book. She is also indebted to Barbara and Peter Bye for their computer assistance.*

# Contents

# *Foreword*

Sister Margherita Marchione is to be commended for offering first-hand information on one of the most important pontificates in world history. Her new book summarizes many of the topics that the general public wishes to have clarified with regard to the life and works of Pope Pius XII.

The book is divided into twelve parts, including moving and convincing sections on Pius XII's virtuous and saintly life. The author has provided new facts and additional testimonials worthy of consideration in his cause for beatification.

Sister Margherita reveals how the people around Pius XII were impressed by his character, inspired by his faith, and moved by his charity and courage. The overwhelming body of evidence should dispel erroneous notions about Pope Pius XII. Sister's book properly moves us away from the mythical image of a silent, cold and unapproachable pontiff to a deeply personable leader who "spoke out" in clear and unmistakable language.

Cardinal Pietro Palazzini, a priest-rescuer honored by Yad Vashem for saving persecuted Jews, wrote in his memoirs (*Il clero e l'occupazione di Roma*): "Amidst the clash of

7

arms, a voice could be heard—the voice of Pius XII. The assistance given to so many people could not have been possible without his moral support, which was much more than quiet consent."

In his address of June 28, 1945 to the Knights of Columbus (published in *Resonare Christum,* Ignatius Press: San Francisco, 1985), Cardinal John Wright said: "The Holy See is the sole international force left on the face of the earth. ... He [Pius XII] remains the voice ... of all those silenced on every side and whose thoughts are thoughts of humanity and brotherhood and peace."

Sister Margherita's books defend the Pope. This new book also celebrates his holy life. I hope it receives the wide readership and impact it deserves.

Reverend Peter Gumpel, SJ

*In his Christmas Eve allocution to the Cardinals, Pope Pius XII referred to the invasion of Poland and related events. (December 26, 1939)*

# Preface

Pope Pius XII was a unique figure in modern history. Throughout his priestly life, he was admired by Catholics and non-Catholics. He practiced Christian virtues heroically, and love of God and neighbor was evident in all his words and actions. His mysticism and spirituality—revealing the unknown depth of his holiness—are shown in his *Last Will and Testament.*

The opinion of many of his contemporaries regarding his spiritual life was that he was a saint. Study of his papal documents will rekindle in the present generation confidence in God, in itself, and in the future. Perhaps his aspirations toward truth and goodness and his extraordinary achievements may be considered one of the great events of our times.

During nineteen years of unprecedented violence and change (1939-1958), Pius XII led the papacy in a ceaseless search for peace. A clear-minded realist with an all-encompassing, mystical sense of human existence, he was in contact with the world's most powerful leaders.

Under Pius XII, the papacy achieved a wider respect than it had had since the Reformation. He won more admiration and praise than any of his pontifical predecessors. He restored Church prestige and provided the faithful and the world with extraordinary leadership.

Today, Pius XII continues to be praised, vilified, judged, and defended. Regarding his posthumous reputation, much of what is widely accepted as true about his life is tinged with the biases of people with a grudge to settle against the Catholic Church. Though one of the most distinguished prelates ever to serve the Church, he may well have been subjected to more unjust criticism than any of his predecessors.

Pius XII spread a culture of solidarity and peace and enriched the lives of his contemporaries by witnessing to the values arising from the Gospel, demonstrating their dynamic fruitfulness and constructing a more just and peaceful society. His sensitivity to emotional and spiritual suffering and his capacity for compassion and love were deeply rooted. He expressed his love by a kind word, a gentle touch, and by blessing everyone as he mingled among them.

During his reign Pius XII received millions of people in public audiences. He went into their midst, talked to them, even heard confessions. Undoubtedly people reacted to these audiences and saw in him a humble, charitable, saintly person. In offering the handshake to so many, his own hands were frequently bruised and scratched. His life reminds the world of his intense love. With total surrender to whatever God asked of him, he wholeheartedly embraced the Will of the Father, living it with great zeal and joy.

The successor of Saint Peter, Pope Pius XII, walked in the shoes of the Fisherman in troubling times, with a faith that did not fail. He was a highly respected twentieth century Church leader whose Christmas messages during and immediately after the Second World War prepared the way for democratic governments throughout much of Europe. In addition, Pius XII spoke out on issues of moral concern and of public policy: these statements laid the foundations for the Second Vatican Council's Constitution *Gaudium et Spes*, the Church in Today's World.

Pope Pius XII's encyclical on the Church as the Mystical Body of Christ, *Mystici Corporis Christi*, 1943, opened the way for a new Catholic approach, to a theology grounded in the insights of both scripture scholars and theologians. The encyclical on biblical studies, *Divino Afflante Spiritu*, issued later in the same year, encouraged students of the written word of God to use fully the fruits of modern research. In *Mediator Dei*, 1947, Pius XII set the stage for the full blossoming of the renewal of Catholic worship based on an accurate understanding of how the Church shaped her life of public prayer from the earliest Christian years. In 1956 he took a first significant step in liturgical reform with the complete revision of the Holy Week Services of the Latin Church.

Pope Pius XII must be credited for having made concrete steps toward the convocation of the Second Vatican Council (1962-1965). He discussed frequently the need for Church reform with Father Riccardo Lombardi, SJ, founder of the *Movement for a Better World,* who helped prepare the strategies used in the development of the Council.

After seeking advice, the Pope studied every issue and was resolute in his decisions. He lived the life of an apostle in poverty and simplicity, was sensitive to the misfortunes of others and supported insults and slanders in silence.

As the public record attests, Pius XII brought to the service of the Church and to humanity his deep commitment to the poor, to the sick and afflicted, and especially to those who suffered because of the ideologies that provoked World War II.

*Pope Pius XII pleaded for relief "to those poor people who are overcome by the sorrows and tribulations of war's calamities." (December 26, 1940)*

# Introduction

Richard Cardinal Cushing once stated that Pope Pius XII was a "theologian, canonist, scholar, linguist, statesman, diplomat. For all of them he has been hailed and praised. But more than anything else he was a pastor, a good shepherd of souls, selflessly dedicated to the honest interests of the Church and to the greater glory of God." He was, indeed, a man on fire with the love of God.

Regardless of one's faith, people in all walks of life and of every religious denomination treasured a meeting with Pius XII. His love was evident in his smiling, affectionate gaze. One day an American actor and his wife were present. As the Pope entered the room, he approached the newlyweds. They recall that "there was electricity in the room when he blessed them." They wished him a happy birthday. His smile lit up the whole room. The Pope gave them medals they would always treasure. "But," said the American actor, "it is Pius XII's simplicity and holiness which will stay with us forever to remind us that it's easy to reach God. He is only a prayer away."

Pope Pius XII was featured on the cover of *Life Magazine* (December 13, 1954) with the words: "The Years of a Great Pope." The photoarticle underlined the fact that the Pope was continuing his efforts to obtain peace in the world. It stated that the world looked back "with pride and admiration at the many-sided career of the churchman who, in his own agonized generation, was already recognized as a great pope. It was the fate of this slender man to know violence intimately, to utter as Pope Pius XII the broken cries for 'peace, peace' on mankind's most murderous century."

Eugenio Pacelli's distinguished 40-year career of diplomatic service for the Church began in 1904 as a research aide in the Office of the Congregation of Extraordinary Ecclesiastical Affairs where he assisted Cardinal Pietro Gasparri in the crucial task of clarifying and updating canon law.

In 1911, Pope Pius X appointed Pacelli Undersecretary for Extraordinary Ecclesiastical Affairs. This department negotiated terms of agreements with foreign governments that would allow the Church to carry out its teaching mission. In 1912, he was appointed its Secretary and then, two years later, Secretary of the Congregation of Extraordinary Ecclesiastical Affairs.

During the early 20th century, the world was plagued with racism, nationalism, and militarism long before Eugenio Pacelli became Pope. When Adolf Hitler was nominated Chancellor of Germany, January 30, 1933, the first official step taken by the Vatican Secretary of State, Cardinal Pacelli, who six years later would become Pope Pius XII, was to defend the Jews. The Holy See sent documents informing the Apostolic Nunzio in Berlin to "officially represent the Vatican defense of the Jews with the German Government and to alert the Nazis about the dangers of antisemitic politics."

As Vatican Secretary of State, Eugenio Pacelli sent sixty protests to Germany between 1933-1939. He worked closely with Pope Pius XI in an effort to combat both Nazism and Communism. German Catholics were warned that Nazism

14

consisted of ideas which no Catholic could accept without denying his faith, To protect them, Pacelli signed the Concordat with Germany on July 20, 1933.

The *New York Times* provides evidence detailing the efforts of the Catholic Church on behalf of the persecuted Jews: "On January 9, 1939, Secretary of State Pacelli sent out messages to the archbishops of the world, instructing them to petition their governments to open their borders to Jews fleeing persecution in Germany. The following day Pacelli wrote to American Cardinals, asking them to assist exiled Jewish professors and scientists."

March 2, 1939—The Western world learned that there was a new Pope. Cardinal Pacelli would now be known as Pope Pius XII. But the next day in Germany, the Nazi newspaper, *Berliner Morgenpost,* wrote: "The election of Cardinal Pacelli is not accepted with favor in Germany because he was always opposed to Nazism."

Herbert L. Matthews, an American journalist in Rome, called Pope Pius XII, "a peacemaker and conciliator" in the *New York Times* (October 15, 1945). During World War II, Pius XII's goodness and spiritual strength impressed the pilgrims who visited him. They recognized his intelligence and his extraordinary capacity to understand the sufferings and the dangers of people everywhere.

Through the Pope's efforts, Rome was treated as an open city. Carlo Sestieri, a Jewish survivor hidden in the Vatican, suggested that "only the Jews who were persecuted understand why the Holy Father could not publicly denounce the Nazi-Fascist government. Without doubt, he helped avoid worse disasters."

No one can claim that enough was done. To claim, however, that Pope Pius XII was indifferent or cowardly, is grave historical falsification. He was a man of peace. In his lifetime, he received more praise and expressions of gratitude from the Jewish people than any other Bishop of Rome in history. Yet, sixty years later, this Pope is burdened down by distortions about his so-called "silence."

How long will scholars condone statements by those who defame Pius XII? Can it be that these attacks are motivated by a desire to discredit the Catholic Church? The increasing slanderous statements by both Jews and Gentiles (including some renegade "Catholics") have nothing really to do with the Holocaust, but have everything to do with the present cultural war. It is an effort to discredit the Church.

According to Jewish historian Pinchas Lapide, the Catholic Church saved between 740,000 and 860,000 Jews from extermination. In Rome alone during the Nazi occupation, 4,447 Jews were hidden in the Vatican at the express wish of the Pope. His "silence" accompanied a powerful action in defense of the Jews: he opened the very doors of the Vatican for Jews to hide there and in Rome's more than 150 ecclesiastical institutions.

The Religious Teachers of Saint Lucy Filippini saved 114 Jews during the Nazi occupation of Rome. Sister Eugenia Befani gave this testimony: "The Sisters assisted Pope Pius XII by preparing and distributing food among the refugees, answering the correspondence of prisoners of war, and saving 114 Jews hidden in three convents in Rome. Sixty were hidden on Via Botteghe Oscure. One evening, while the Jews were having dinner, the doorbell rang and a Nazi soldier asked if any Jews were living there. Sister flatly told him that no Jews were in the convent. Reluctantly and apparently unconvinced, the soldier left. Would he return? As a precautionary measure, Sister hurried to the Jews and told them to hide. Immediately the Jews disappeared. They were terrorized. A pregnant woman was so frightened that she

16

was having severe pains. The Sisters secretly rushed her to a hospital where, prematurely, she gave birth to a beautiful girl."

Only a person unfamiliar with a totalitarian regime could criticize a leader for failing to encourage open rebellion. In Nazi Germany active resistance meant immediate arrest, usually death. Most people could not communicate by telephone, post, or messenger; it was dangerous to speak openly even to trusted friends who might be arrested and tortured; they knew that nineteen guilllotines executed an estimated fifty people daily.

The following letter from Anthony D. Lutz (April 4, 2003) confirms these facts: "Any Catholic who resisted Hitler was jailed or killed. I lived in Germany in the early 1960s. There a church organist told me, he had to hide the parish church's youth flag because Hitler wanted them confiscated. A former sacristan at Cologne Cathedral told me the Gestapo was waiting in the sacristy to question the preacher after his Sunday sermon. The secretary of Germany's Bishops' Conference told me he would never write a book about Catholic resistance during Hitler's regime because no one would believe him. He (Monsignor Abel from Fulda) was interrogated forty-three times by the Gestapo. They opened all his mail, listened to all his telephone conversations, and he was tailed by the Gestapo wherever he drove around Germany.

"A Franciscan Provincial told me that one of his priests, a famous Classical scholar, was turned in by a young lady who overheard him criticize Hitler. As punishment and to intimidate everyone else, this priest was beheaded. When I visited my Dad's village in Bavaria, a distant cousin told me that in the little town of 1200 citizens, no one knew who the spy was. Everyone was spied on. A sister and brother by the name of Scholl at the University of Munich were caught publishing articles against Hitler. They were given a perfunctory trial and then guillotined. Their story was told in a book entitled, *The White Rose*. Ask yourself honestly, what could you do during that period and survive?"

The Vatican was a neutral state. Faithful to the Lateran Treaty, Pius XII remained impartial. He prudently asked the American Bishops to issue a public statement: "…We feel a deep sense of revulsion against the cruel indignities heaped upon the Jews… We raise our voice in protest against despotic tyrants who have lost all sense of humanity by condemning thousands of innocent persons to death in subjugated countries, by placing thousands of innocent victims in concentration camps, and by permitting unnumbered persons to die of starvation."

Cardinal Pietro Palazzini wrote in his memoirs.: "Amidst the clash of arms, a voice could be heard—the voice of Pius XII. The assistance given to so many people could not have been possible without his moral support, which was much more than quiet consent"( *Il clero e l'occupazione di Roma*, 1995, p. 16). In 1985, Palazzini was honored by Israel's Yad Vashem as a "Righteous Gentile." He explicitly stated that Pius XII ordered him to save Jews.

In Castelgandolfo thousands of Jews and other refugees were saved during World War II. One photograph, with tapestry in the background that clearly depicts the papal coat-of-arms, shows seven women and ten children in the Pope's private apartment. These rooms served as a nursery where many Jewish babies were born.

Numerous documents confirm that Pope Pius XII was indeed a champion of peace, freedom, human dignity; a pastor who encouraged Catholics to look on Christians and Jews as their brothers and sisters in Christ, all children of a common Father. He was a witness of love, and the Servant of the servants of God.

It suffices to study the testimonials given by contemporaries who heard his words. He spoke of freedom, education, economic and social problems. He left us a legacy that offers valid evidence of his ecumenism. Indeed, he spoke of brotherhood, of love, and of peace among religious groups. His message was a source of inspiration. He was a sacred messenger, who tried to unite and to bring peace to the world. In a period of spiritual poverty and material destruction, his words of wisdom and indefatigable works translated, as no other person, the message of Christ.

Eugenio Pacelli was Nunzio in Germany (1917-1929), then Vatican Secretary of State (1930-1939) and finally elected Pope (1939-1958). He bequeathed to posterity an abundance of writings and discourses in every field of endeavor. No previous religious leader had ever written on a variety of topics other than religious ones.

With the publication of his writings, it is now possible to understand the breadth and the importance of his words. A series of texts preceded his pontificate: A *Collection of Discourses* (Berlin, 1930) when he was Apostolic Nunzio in Germany; *Discourses and Sermons 1931-1939*, (Vatican, Tipografia Poliglotta, 1939) given as Secretary of State. More important from a political and religious point of view are the following: *Discourses and Radio Messages* (Vatican, Tipografia Poliglotta, 1940-1959) in 20 volumes; *Acts and Discourses* by Pius XII (Rome, Edizioni Paoline, 1940-1959), in 20 volumes.

During the Second Vatican Council, Pius XII is quoted more than any other writer except the Sacred Scriptures. His words served the Council Fathers and show the breadth of his theology and his understanding of the needs of the

Church in the twentieth century. His numerous encyclicals embrace every field of endeavor: religion, government, social reform.

Pius XII promoted biblical studies; denounced the errors of racism and totalitarianism; attacked national socialism; addressed moral questions that affect married life; defended the rights of women to participate in the social and political life of the world; addressed the Italian Catholic Union of Midwives and the National Congress of the Family Front, as well as the Fifth International Congress on Psychotherapy and Clinical Psychology; and explained the moral questions involved in Radio, TV and Motion Pictures.

He warned against minimizing the importance of dogma and defined the dogma of the Assumption; exhorted the clergy of the entire world on the development of holiness in Priestly Life; addressed the Second World Congress of the Lay Apostolate and the Second General Congress, which tightened the bonds uniting organizations among themselves and with the Holy See; promoted Catholic Missions and urged Catholics to adhere more strictly to Catholic life and principles.

Pius XII was the first Pope who left such an abundance of writings and discourses. The following excerpt, written by hand, was part of a discourse to an international group of doctors: "How exalted, how worthy of all honour is the character of your profession! The doctor has been appointed by God Himself to minister to the needs of suffering humanity. He who created that fever-consumed or mangled frame, now in your hands, who loves it with an eternal love, confided to you the ennobling charge of restoring it to health. You will bring to the sick-room and the operating table something of the charity of God, of the love and tenderness of Christ, the Master Physician of soul and body. That the blessing of the King of Kings may descend upon you and your work and all your dear ones and your beloved country and remain forever, is the wish and prayer that rises from Our affectionate heart."

Throughout his life Pacelli continued scholarly pursuits. In 1943, for example, in a discourse to the Pontifical Academy of Science, he forecast the development of atomic energy and discussed the disintegration which uranium undergoes when bombarded by neutrons. The Pope expressed the hope that its force would be harnessed for the service of man and not released for his destruction.

On September 19, 1945, the *New York Times* wrote: "Pope Pius XII this morning received Sir Alexander Fleming and discussed with him new uses of penicillin. The discoverer of penicillin presented the Pontiff a plate for cultivating mold to be used in research. Sir Alexander, after a twenty-minute audience, declared he was astonished at the Pope's knowledge of his discovery."

In 1951 Pius XII spoke on modern science and the proofs for the existence of God. He had a sincere predilection for the medical profession: "Like the priest and the Church, a doctor must be a friend and must help humanity; he must be a true collaborator of God in the defense and development of creation."

In his last discourse to surgeons, five days before his death, he continued to teach them the value and the beauty of one's soul: "How many souls found serenity in your capable hands! How many were helped by your science and art! Always recognize that your mission can and must go beyond the body and teach those entrusted to you to appreciate interior beauty."

Pius XII held private or general audiences for people in all walks of life. Addressing each group, he reminded them of their duties and obligations and had extraordinary insight into all types of problems. To bankers the Pope cautioned that money is not an end in itself, but merely an instrument to be used justly for securing the God-given rights of all. To midwives he clarified the Church's continued stand against abortion and contraceptive practices. He recalled that this is not just Catholic teaching. It is rooted in the natural law, the rules of Creation as God made the world. He not only showed his appreciation of good craftsmanship as he spoke to jewelers, but told streetcar conductors that he understood their vexations on the job. They knew he was urging them to acquire the virtue of patience. To athletes he said that the important thing about sports is that it develops will power and Christian domination of the body, as well as "elevates the spirit above small-mindedness, dishonesty, and trickery."

*The Oxford Dictionary of Popes* states that, on May 3, 1939, Pius XII called for "an international conference to settle differences peacefully" (p. 319). He outlined the kind of order necessary for peace: it must respect the independent rights of all nations and also of minorities; it must provide for progressive disarmament; it must provide a supreme world juridical authority with power to revise treaties.

Pope Pius XII was a person who radiated an interior peace and a spiritual beauty that inspired everyone. He was endowed with great sensitivity and a spirit of brotherhood. During a period in history full of lies, desperation and hatred, he was an exceptional and saintly individual, a symbol of mercy, hope and love.

*Pope Pius XII spoke of "those who, because of their nationality or their descent, are pursued by mounting misfortune and increasing suffering." (June 2, 1943)*

# Part I: Eugenio Pacelli

Marcantonio Pacelli was Vatican Undersecretary of the Interior. He had seven children, of whom the third son was Filippo, who married Virginia Graziosi. They had four children. The oldest, Francesco, was a brilliant Vatican attorney who helped negotiate the Lateran Treaty with Italy in 1929. Pope Pius XI was pleased with the way the Treaty was written and stated: "We have given back God to Italy and Italy to God." Catholics throughout the world agreed with this assessment. There were two daughters, Giuseppina and Elisabetta. Their second son and third child, Eugenio, became Pope Pius XII.

Eugenio Maria Giuseppe Giovanni Pacelli was born in Rome, March 2, 1876, and baptized two days later, according to the records at the Church of Saints Celso and Giuliano. He was baptized by his uncle, Monsignor Giuseppe Pacelli. His godparents were his maternal uncle Filippo Graziosi and paternal aunt Teresa Pacelli.

A few years later, the Pacellis moved to Via della Vetrina, 20. At age four Eugenio was enrolled in the kindergarten and elementary school conducted by the Sisters of Divine Providence. Eugenio enjoyed a childhood in deeply religious surroundings. In the apartment there was a shrine of the Madonna with a prie-dieu where he would kneel in prayer.

23

Eugenio was a precocious, sensitive and impressionable child. He was deeply attentive as he listened to his mother commenting on the lives of the saints and the early martyrs of the Church. One day, his uncle, Monsignor Giuseppe Pacelli, told him the story of a missionary priest who was persecuted and finally crucified by his tormentors. Eugenio told his uncle, that he too would like to be a martyr, "but— without the nails."

After kindergarten and elementary school, Eugenio began his studies at the Ennio Quirino Visconti Lyceum. When classes at the Lyceum were over each day, young Eugenio would wait for his brother Francesco in the Church of the Gesù. One day Eugenio was late coming home from school. His mother found him in this church, kneeling before the beautiful ancient painting known as "La Madonna della Strada." Questioned by his mother about why he was there so long, he said simply, "I talk to our Lady. I tell her everything!"

At the Lyceum Eugenio established a close friendship with a Jewish schoolmate, Guido Mendes. The boys visited each other's home and shared common interests. Still vivid in 1958 in the elderly Mendes' memory was his classmate Eugenio who defended the Church. He described Eugenio as the leading student and a careful dresser, always wearing a coat and tie. "He was always winning academic prizes," Mendes recalled. He also stated that when the Fascists began to threaten Jews in Italy, the then Secretary of State Pacelli helped the Mendes family flee to Jerusalem. They remained in touch with one another over the years.

Summers were spent at Pacelli's home in Onano, where he liked to ride his horse. He was also a good swimmer in Lake Bolsena and a swift canoeist. As a hiker he had the reputation of being unbeatable. He maintained a collection of coins and stamps, had an ardent interest in archaeology, and enjoyed playing the violin. Records show that Eugenio possessed a photographic memory and graduated with highest honors. After a four-day retreat, Pacelli announced to his family that he would not follow family tradition and become a lawyer, but that he intended to become a priest.

In 1894, at age 18, Eugenio entered the Capranica Seminary and enrolled at the Gregorian University. From childhood he was afflicted with stomach difficulties and showed signs of tuberculosis. Pope Leo XIII came to his rescue and he was given permission to live at home while taking courses at the Sapienza School of Philosophy and Letters, as well as at the Papal Athenaeum of Saint Apollinaris for Theology. Pacelli received his Baccalaureate and Licentiate degrees *summa cum laude*. The day after he was ordained on Easter Sunday, April 2, 1899, he celebrated his first Mass in the Borghese Chapel of the Basilica of Saint Mary Major, in Rome.

The young Pacelli made rapid progress in his career because he was brilliant, conscientious and hardworking. It was only in obedience to higher authority that he entered the diplomatic service of the Holy See. In 1929, when his task as Apostolic Nuncio had come to an end, he desired to become a diocesan bishop and do pastoral work. Instead, he became Vatican Secretary of State. Later, elected Pope, he did not accept his election immediately, but insisted on another ballot. When this was overwhelmingly in his favor, he accepted the election as a sign of God's will, but "in signum crucis," as a heavy cross.

Throughout his life, Eugenio Pacelli worked for peace. The name "Pacelli" suggests peace and he selected as the motto on his crest the words, *opus justitiae pax*. In 1936, as Secretary of State, he came to the United States and made an in-depth study of the American Church. During his "unofficial" visit, Cardinal Pacelli appealed to the United States to throw open its doors to Jewish refugees, but his request went unheeded. On November 5, 1936, the eve of his return, President Franklin D. Roosevelt—who two days earlier had a landslide victory for a second term—invited him to a luncheon at his home in Hyde Park, New York.

Although he preferred pastoral work, Eugenio Pacelli seemed destined for a diplomatic career and served the Church under four Popes: Leo XIII, Saint Pius X, Benedict XV and Pius XI. Then, for almost two decades, from March 2, 1939 to his death, he was entrusted with the keys of supreme jurisdiction given to the Prince of the Apostles: "Thou art Peter and upon this rock I will build My Church."

Pope Pius XII's 1957 Christmas message ended with these words: "*Peace* is a 'good' so precious, so desirable and so desired that every effort to defend it, even at the cost of sacrificing one's own aspirations, is a 'good' well spent." His last public word was *Peace*. On October 5, 1958, he ended his discourse to the members of the Latin Notary Congress exhorting his audience to do its duty with regard to the "conservation of *Peace*, which is desired by all men of good will."

On Monday, October 6, 1958, Pius XII suddenly collapsed while working at his desk. Two days later he had a second stroke. On Thursday, October 9, 1958, the Pope suffered a heart attack and died. Prayers re-echoed throughout the world. Tears were shed by millions of faithful.

People in every walk of life had been inspired by him. Men, women and children of every persuasion had visited him in the Vatican. His enthusiastic bright eyes, combined with brisk step and swift movements were contagious. His personal magnetism was a blend of casualness and dignity, warmth and affection, compassion and humor. His food was frugal and limited as he dined alone while reading the newspapers at breakfast and reviewing official papers submitted by his secretaries during other meals. Though born an aristocrat, he was an ascetic.

On March 18, 1979, forty years after Cardinal Eugenio Pacelli became Pope, John Paul II recalled: "I shall never forget the profound impression which I felt when I saw him close-up for the first time. It was during an audience which he granted to the young priests and seminarians of the Belgian College. Pius came to each one and when he reached me the College Rector (Monsignor Fürstenberg) told him that I came from Poland. The Pope stopped for a while and repeated with evident emotion 'from Poland'; then he said in Polish 'Praised be Jesus Christ.' This was in the first months of the year 1947, less than two years after the end of the Second World War, which had been a terrible trial for Europe, especially for Poland. On the fortieth anniversary of the beginning of this important pontificate we cannot forget the contribution that Pius XII made to the theological preparation for the Second Vatican Council, especially by his teachings on the Church, by the first liturgical reforms, by the new impetus he gave to biblical studies and by his great attention to the problems of the contemporary world." (General audience of April 28, 1999.)

At the start of his 1987 visit to the United States, John Paul II defended Pius XII during a meeting with Jewish leaders. He extended an invitation for all, Jews and Gentiles, to be united spiritually: "I hope that at the dawn of the third millennium sincere dialogue between Christians and Jews will help create a new civilization founded on the one, holy and merciful God, and fostering a humanity reconciled in love."

This is what his predecessor, Eugenio Pacelli, attempted to accomplish during and after World War II. Regardless of race or religion, whoever approached His Holiness was overwhelmed with sentiments of filial devotion and deep veneration. People did not envision Pacelli the Man, but Pacelli, the Vicar of Christ in the fullness of his mission. With acute wisdom and courage, Pope Pius XII dominated the tempest of his day and age, disseminated the truth of the divine law, and endeavored to restore love among all peoples.

# Part II: A Virtuous Life

Pope Pius XI recognized the goodness and virtue of his Secretary of State, Cardinal Eugenio Pacelli. He appreciated his keen intelligence and his capacity to radiate an interior peace and spiritual beauty. On several occasions he sent him to countries as papal representative, and encouraged him to accept an invitation to visit the USA.

Pius XII was endowed with the gifts of the Holy Spirit and, to a heroic degree, with all the virtues, theological and cardinal. He was a prayerful, serene, tranquil individual, dedicated to his every duty as Pontiff. By his very nature, he was a meek and timid individual and preferred a quiet and serene atmosphere; sweetness versus severity, persuasion versus imposition. He was an orator and prepared himself conscientiously for each discourse. Then, without notes, he would improvise and abandon himself to his inspiration.

Very humble and truthful, he considered others equally so. As he frequently prepared his own documents, he would eliminate expressions he felt were too strong and insert more gentle phrases. He wanted everyone to be satisfied when they asked for favors, concessions or dispensations and found it difficult to refuse the persistent demands of some people. However, during important discussions he was not timid and was always ready to respond clearly.

As Pope, he was known to ponder over his decisions and never obliged anyone to accept a nomination. He merely made it known that it would please him. In all his words and actions, he was guided by his love of God, his devotion to Our Lady and his concept of the dignity of the Papacy. He protected the Church and, for many years, diligently worked with learned churchmen to prepare for the Second Vatican Council.

For the love of God and of the countless people whom he touched with his compassion, Pius XII willingly accepted the interior "dark night of the soul." He remained faithful to his duties and supported all trials as he continued his intense prayer life. His trust in God enabled him to advance along the path to holiness despite the many trials and calumnies. During the papal audiences, his faith, his hope and his love for all was felt by millions of faithful who were inspired by his fatherly concern, his smiling face, his inspiring words. Repeatedy he called on Our Lady, to whom he was especially devoted from childhood. He assured everyone of his prayers and embraced the whole world in imitation of Christ on the Cross who, burdened with the iniquities of humanity, cried out, "My God, my God, why have you abandoned me?"

Pius XII worked with great devotion for peace; condemned Nazism prior to and during hostilities; alleviated the suffering and saved the lives of Jewish and Christian war victims.

A few months after Pope Pius XII's death, a prayer with the *imprimatur* of Bishop Peter Canisius, Vicar General of Vatican City, was soon circulated among the faithful: "O Jesus, eternal High Priest, who didst deign to raise Thy faithful servant, Pius XII, to the supreme dignity of Thy Vicar on earth and to grant him the grace to be a fearless defender of the faith, a valiant champion of justice and peace, zealous in proclaiming the glory of Thy most holy Mother, a shining example of charity and all virtues, deign now to grant us, in view of his merits, the graces we ask of Thee; so that, made certain of his efficacious intercession with Thee, we may one day see him raised to the honors of our altars, Amen."

A Petition asking His Holiness Pope John Paul II to expedite the beatification of Pope Pius XII was circulated and the signatures of thousands of people from all parts of the world were deposited in the Vatican. The Petition reads:

"With profound respect and sincere devotion, We, the undersigned, humbly request that the cause for the beatification of Pope Pius XII proceed without delay. Pius XII's virtuous life speaks for itself and is supported by an abundance of incontestable documentary evidence. The truth regarding his service to the Church and the World, as a diplomat and during his pontificate, prior to and through the World War II period, is also historically established. He has been the victim of an unjust smear campaign for fifty years. Now, however, overwhelming evidence has been amassed that proves beyond doubt that he labored without pause for peace, that he sought to assist in every way possible the victims of war, especially Jews, hundreds of thousands of whom were spared through his efforts, and that he constantly warned the world of the horrors of Nazism and Communism. We urge that you honor this holy and brave Pontiff at the soonest possible date."

Millions of visitors to the Vatican experienced intense faith, hope and love of God and of neighbor. They were inspired by Pope Pius XII's fatherly concern, his smiling face, his inspiring words.

# Faith

Faith is the foundation stone of all the virtues. Without faith, it is impossible to please God. From his youth and throughout his life, love of God was Eugenio Pacelli's strength and inspiration. He was a pious child, served as an altar boy and visited the Shrine of the "Madonna della Strada" every day. He was an excellent student and his knowledge increased in all fields. When called to the priesthood, his spiritual life was enhanced by his theological studies.

Early on he defended and protected the Faith. His teachings on the Catholic Faith were indispensable for the development of Vatican II. He seemed predestined to become the Vicar of Christ. In fact, Pius XI recommended him not only because of his natural gifts, but because he had a spirit of prayer and sacrifice.

Every word and every gesture during the Eucharistic Liturgy revealed his Faith, his humility, his piety. He was devoted to the Blessed Sacrament, to the Sacred Heart, to the passion of Jesus, to Our Lady, Saint Joseph, the Angels. Each day, he celebrated the Holy Mass with great faith, recited the Breviary, spent at least two hours in meditation before the Blessed Sacrament, with daily examination of conscience, spiritual reading, visits to the Blessed Sacrament, and the Rosary.

# Hope

The virtue of hope enhanced and strengthened the quality of Pius XII's life and gave him total confidence in the mercy of God. With David, he could say: "What do I want on this earth, if not You, O God of my heart's longing, my treasure for all eternity!" He worked for the glory of God and the good of souls. He understood human frailty and had deep Christian optimism.

During the most tragic moments of his pontificate, he was serene and trusted in God's goodness. This was communicated to all who approached him. While he suffered intensely because of the spiritual and material conditions in the Church, he gave comfort and hope to people of all faiths. He was not discouraged during the most difficult moments of the war years.

His hope was shown during his illness especially during the period prior to his death. He desired to be with God, had faith in divine grace and was resigned to the Will of God.

## *Charity*

Even as a child, love of God was ever foremost in Eugenio Pacelli's thoughts. He appreciated the gift of life and avoided all sin as he progressed in the spiritual life. He wanted to make known God's goodness toward humanity and his only purpose in life was to contribute to the Kingdom of God. Very reserved, he did not speak about his personal spirituality, but whoever approached him would realize that he was in constant union with God.

Cardinal Domenico Tardini wrote: "Often the Church bells would ring at noon during our discussions. Immediately Pius XII would stand, fold his hands, lower his eyes and begin to recite the *Angelus Domini*."

When he prayed, but also in his actions and in the governance of Vatican affairs, one would always note Pius XII's profound union with God, as well as his love for the Madonna and the Saints. Whoever had the opportunity to be with him was convinced of his nobility of soul and recognized that he was intimately united with God whose presence was visible.

He visited the Blessed Sacrament in his chapel several times each day. Kneeling and praying it seemed as though the external world did not exist. During the most tragic moments of his pontificate, he accepted the Cross while suffering intensely because of the lack of understanding and the calumnies that were showered on him. But he never became discouraged and continued to trust in God's help. He bore the grave illnesses in 1954 and 1958 for the love of God and accepted the pain and the anguish with an heroic spirit. Often he repeated the *Anima Christi* and other ejaculations.

Pius XII's charity toward his neighbor was constant. He could not dedicate himself directly to the Apostolate because obedience required that he devote his time to study and to diplomacy. Whenever he could perform his priestly ministry during free moments—preaching, confessing, advising and helping the poor—he experienced the joy of the priesthood.

As Nuncio in Bavaria, he frequently visited prison camps, distributed food and clothing, and concerned himself with the spiritual needs of the prisoners. As Secretary of State, he prepared his own sermons and preached in various churches at weddings and on feastdays to honor the Saints and the Blessed Virgin Mary. During his vacations in Rorschach (Switzerland), he performed all his priestly duties. Much of his time was spent seeking peace, alleviating sufferings, satisfying the needs of those requesting help during the war, and dedicating himself to the care of souls.

Especially during his pontificate, Pope Pius XII was an extraordinary example of charity, the living model of a true shepherd of souls, teaching future pastors to accomplish their apostolate by words and actions. He gave them specific instructions: "Enlighten the minds, direct the consciences, comfort and sustain souls who are doubtful and sorrowful. Your zeal must be strengthened by charity."

## *Justice*

Lover of truth, Pius XII did everything possible to promote justice in his rapport with nations and during his countless audiences, as well as through official documents and formal discourses.

Pius XII's righteousness and honesty were such that no one could ever doubt his integrity. More than with words and exhortations, he stimulated his collaborators with the example of his dedication to work, his rectitude in all affairs, his fidelity to God and to the Church. He tried to improve the condition of the oppressed; he tried to assure for all classes a way of life conforming to the dignity of the individual. He defended the rights of the Church through official or non-official ways, especially through Concordats with various governments.

When Eugenio Pacelli became Pope, he ordered that the expenses of his private apartment be paid with his personal patrimony. He was attentive to the needs of Vatican employees and to the administration of the Vatican State. All were treated fairly with compassion and goodness.

As Supreme Pontiff he was indefatigable, working day and night to promote the spiritual and temporal good of all humanity. His efforts during World War I and II are well known. His radio messages and discourses fill twenty volumes. He was Pope Pius XI's representative in Buenos Aires and in France. When the safety of Jews was threatened during the occupation of Rome by the Nazis, he opened the doors of convents and monasteries to shelter them. When the Allies bombed Rome, he was the first to assist the poor and the suffering.

Throughout his life, he appreciated the efforts and the assistance of his collaborators. He was tactful and delicate; he demanded much of himself and of others. Until the very end, he had zeal and charity for all, including his own family, but he avoided every form of nepotism. He had little contact with his family during his pontificate because he had to use all his time in the service of the Church. However, he never failed to remember their feastdays and to pray for them. At his death, the Vatican was the beneficiary of his entire estate.

## *Prudence*

Pius XII's penetrating intelligence permitted him to see clearly the nature and aspects of problems and the consequences that would be the result of his decisions. He was always prudent and did not make hasty decisions. His extraordinary memory helped him to recall priceless examples and teachings of the past; his innate delicacy and human understanding made him foresee possible psychological reactions to his decisions; his profound faith and his Christian charity animated him, and placed him in a position to follow the Will of God.

Pius XII practiced the virtue of prudence. He carefully studied the circumstances of the issue, reflected seriously and prayed before coming to a decision. He always had before him ample documentation and sought information about people and things that would enlighten him. Only then, after careful consideration would he commit himself regarding the issue. His circumspection and prudence was noted as, with great humility, he would submit problems to the judgment of competent scholars, even seeking advice from those holding opposite opinions. If solid documentation proved him to be lacking in information, he was always ready to accept another's opinion and revise his writings, including the new information in his final version. He would correct his own proofs of important documents after verifying each reference that was suggested.

Even when he had to approve nominations for various offices, he studied the *curriculum vitae* of each candidate with great care because he felt it was his duty and responsibility to protect the Church from criticism and damage to its reputation. The large quantity of *Acts, Discourses, Encyclicals* and other writings demonstrate the prudence of his words and actions. But he was always spontaneous and cordial and earned the unconditional admiration of diplomats, and all who worked with him in the governance of the Vatican. For fifteen years of his pontificate he spoke without a manuscript. In his conversations and audiences, he united prudence with human cordiality. His benevolence, love and interest in the personal needs of others were acknowledged.

Eugenio Pacelli's prudence was so exemplary and so appreciated that people from all walks of life sought his counsel. Both Pope Pius XI and Cardinal Gasparri respected his opinion. As Pope, he acted prudently. Doing everything with moderation, discretion and delicacy, he was always guided by faith, hope and charity—principles that regulate every Christian life. The exercise of all these virtues was balanced and harmonious, even during the most difficult times of his life. One must truly recognize his heroic prudence.

# Temperance

Those who worked closely with Pius XII have attested to the fact that he lived a life of exemplary temperance and mortification. He was an ascetic and practiced every virtue in an extraordinary way. He wanted only simple food. His meals were that of a poor person. He ate very little, did not use alcoholic beverages except a small glass of wine mixed with water during meals. Whenever there was an official dinner, everyone noticed his dignified and spiritual manner of eating and drinking with temperance and mortification.

He did not use tobacco nor eat desserts. Even though he needed special foods, during the war years he forbade any exceptions for his own meals. He refused to drink coffee because others could not have it. His weight was reduced to fifty-seven "kilos."

He did not want his apartment heated because the thousands of refugees hidden by the Vatican could not have their rooms heated. He slept only four hours each day, after working until two in the morning and getting up at six a.m. Even when the time period for fasting in order to receive Holy Communion was lessened, he continued to observe the original fast regulations.

# Fortitude

Pius XII's fortitude may be seen in his complete dedication to his office, his life of mortification, his perfect discipline in exercising this virtue. He had a meek character and pleasant disposition, combined with a strength of purpose that enabled him to make important decisions for the Church. He did not hesitate to accomplish the arduous task of guiding the Church for almost twenty years of his pontificate.

He introduced reforms and renovations in the Church which were strengthened by his successors. It suffices to recall his heroic support of the needy and persecuted during World War II and subsequent years. In his decisions he was never guided by a desire for popularity; his rectitude and fortitude did not allow any one to influence what he felt was his duty in promoting the good of souls entrusted to his care. Frequently misunderstood, maligned and criticized, he acted according to his conscience and supported the trials with resignation and patience. In the last analysis he was indifferent to what others said of him, provided he could do God's Will.

Pius XII did not fear death and was ready to sacrifice his life in defending the rights of the Church and fulfilling his pastoral duties. After World War I, when revolutionaries penetrated the Nunciature in Monaco (Baveria) and tried to break open the Archives, Nuncio Pacelli fearlessly stood in front of them, ignoring the pistol that was held against his chest. He demanded calmly that the intruders leave the premises immediately, and they did.

During World War II, Pius XII was advised not to go too close to the German soldiers during general audiences for fear of being killed. Nevertheless, he refused to use any precautionary measures and continued to approach the Germans, talk to them and bless them. Some of them confided in His Holiness who responded with goodness and courtesy, giving them spiritual advice. He spoke perfect German and from their accent, could tell them the region from which they came. After the audience many of them wrote to their families, pleased to have spoken to the Pope. They repeated his words, adding that he was very gentle and good. The military censorship was not very pleased to read the favorable remarks and therefore forbade the German soldiers to visit the Vatican.

Word spread that the Nazis intended to capture and deport Pius XII. When he learned that plans were being implemented to insure his safety, he stated clearly that he would not leave the Vatican and that he would have to be taken by them physically. He also refused to go to air-raid shelters; instead he remained in his chapel in prayer. During the bombing of Rome, he left the Vatican to help the suffering and wounded, to comfort them and assist them both spiritually and materially. He never feared for his life and, abandoning himself to the Will of God, accepted with admirable resignation and Christian fortitude, the atrocious suffering during his sickness.

Pius XII did not fear criticism, opposition or accusations. He was courageous and fearless when confronted by Nazism, Fascism and Communism and declared that he would continue his duties as Pope when word came that he would be taken to a German concentration camp. When he learned that the clergy and the faithful were imprisoned, churches closed or profaned, and liberty destroyed in the occupied lands, he definitely denounced the Nazis. In the midst of these injustices, he spoke with the competency of Judge, with the authority of the Divine Master, with the love of the Father. "The Church," he said, "stands serene and calm, but resolute and ready to fight every attack. As a good, tender, and charitable mother, the Church does not seek battle; but because she is a mother and seeks to defend the dignity, integrity, life, liberty, honor and eternal salvation of her children, she is firm, indomitable, irremovable, not with material forces but with the moral strength of her love." (*Discorsi*, Vol. VIII, pp. 105-106.)

# Poverty

In imitation of Christ, whose Vicar he was, Pius XII continued to live a life of simplicity. Although he possessed a substantial inheritance, he did not seek improvements and comforts in the papal apartment. Personal expenses and those for the upkeep of his apartment were paid from his patrimony. Offerings to Pius XII were given directly to the Secretariat of State and gifts that remained in his apartment were bequeathed to the Holy See. When Pius XII moved to the papal apartment, he told the architect during renovations to avoid every appearance of luxury. In Castelgandolfo, his summer residence, he insisted there be no improvements. One summer he was made aware of the air-conditioning improvements in a section of the Vatican. He was informed that, since his apartment was directly under the roof of the Apostolic Palace and exposed to the sun, air-conditioning would be provided so that he would be better able to work. His answer was that "work with mortification had more value." Taking advantage of the occasion, he reiterated forcefully that he wished to live like the poor who could not have such luxury. The apartment was not air-conditioned. He never lamented about the summer heat or the bitter winter months.

Pius XII knew he was only the administrator of Church goods. While he practiced poverty with regard to food, clothing, living quarters, he was particularly generous to the poor during the war and the period of reconstruction. He even suggested that some of the Vatican treasures be sold, but was told that the results would be insufficient to provide for the needs created by the war. Instead, he utilized his personal patrimony to the extent that it was necessary to warn him there would be no funds left for his coffin. He answered that his administrator would have to ask a benefactor to provide one.

Pius XII was not attached to worldly goods and made no effort to increase his own patrimony. He disposed of the gifts he received. After his brother's death, he gave a bishop his pectoral cross, in which there was an amethyst of great value that had been on his mother's ring. He had received the cross at his consecration as bishop. His wardrobe was simple and modest. The Sisters who cared for him mended his clothing. Everything was totally consumed. His shoes had to be worn out before he would accept a replacement. He wanted the liturgical functions in Saint Peter's Basilica, however, to have all the splendor and pomp that was needed to honor God. When he died, he left all his possessions to the Apostolic See.

## *Chastity*

Pius XII frequently wrote and spoke about the nobility of consecrated life: its importance for the life of the Church, for the sanctification of individuals. Chaste from his youth, he maintained his celibacy and remained pure of heart under the protection of the Blessed Virgin Mary whom he venerated dearly. Consequently, as a truly consecrated soul, he cultivated a sense of modesty, reverence, and purity which permeated his whole being.

Love of God and of neighbor, profound union with God, his intense spirit of prayer, his desire to imitate the poverty, mortification and passion of Jesus Christ were an intimate part of his life. There is no trace of any imperfection with regard to his vow of virginity.

## Obedience

Even in childhood, Eugenio Pacelli was obedient and disciplined. He was devoted to his family and lived a virtuous life. He followed the directives of his spiritual director throughout his life, both in the seminary and during his early diplomatic career. He performed his duties faithfully. His superiors always appreciated his frankness and sincerity. As Secretary of State, he was a faithful, prudent and humble servant of the Church and, as Pope, his zeal increased and he continued to serve the Church.

Pius XII respected what his predecessors had ordained, observing liturgical rubrics and the rules of fast and abstinence even after they were changed. His zeal never diminished. His dedication to the Church was heroic. His obedience to the Will of God and of the Church was perfect.

## Humility

Saint Peter tells us that "God resists the proud and gives his grace to the humble." Already at age thirteen, Eugenio Pacelli wrote a self-portrait which demonstrated his sincerity and humility. In the essay he described the positive and negative aspects of his own personality. Although he knew he had gifts of intelligence and memory, of firm will power, of prayerfulness and special graces, he was not proud. He was conscious of his deficiencies and attributed his success to the Lord. He did not seek promotions and ecclesiastical honors. His ideal was to dedicate himself to the poor and abandoned. When Pacelli received a telegram in Berlin that he was made a Cardinal, he was disappointed and remarked spontaneously: "But I begged my brother to try to stop this promotion!"

During his vacations in Switzerland or while walking in the Vatican gardens he was at home with little children who confided in him. When he contacted a flu-like illness and desperately needed rest and care, arrangements were made for him to recuperate in a convent in Einseideln, Switzerland. Gradually he regained his health. One day, while walking to a village near the convent, he met a little boy crying and tried to console him. He learned that the toddler had lost money his mother had given him to buy bread. The Nuncio dried the youngster's tears, bought the bread, and walked the child home. Soon after, though not fully recovered, the Nuncio felt strong enough to resume his duties of helping others in Munich.

His interest in the poor was constant. In Germany he worked with prisoners as well as the poor. His humility was seen through his actions for he did not seek his own glory but the good of souls and the glory of God. He never credited himself for the work he accomplished in the name of his predecessor; instead, he attributed everything to the Pontiff himself. Always humble, he willingly accepted the advice given when well-documented and often laughed at his own foibles. As Pope he was embarrassed by the manifestations of filial devotion showered on him. He did not like to be photographed. Only when he learned that it was for the benefit of the faithful and that this was part of his apostolate, he conceded and patiently submitted to the wishes of the faithful. He was humiliated and mortified when he had to appear with great solemnity and pomp.

After the war, Pius XII wanted to donate a small vehicle to several pastors of Rome who were in dire need of transportation. On one occasion, when he went to the courtyard to bless them, he was embarrassed to see the small vehicles next to his large car. Only when he was told that no pastor would appreciate his car because it was already twenty years old and was in need of repairs, did he feel comforted. Having a sense of evangelical poverty, in his humility he refused to substitute his old car for a more efficient one.

Pius XII was occupied day and night in the fulfillment of his duties. Animated, perhaps, by the title of his office as "Servant of the Servants of God," he was convinced of his own nothingness. On the occasion of the fortieth anniversary of his episcopal consecration, the Pope asked for prayers, observing that often the faithful did not realize the terrible responsibility he had, and confessing that he trembled at the thought of God's judgment.

During World War II, Pius XII's goodness and spiritual strength inspired the pilgrims who visited him. They recognized his intelligence and his extraordinary capacity to understand the sufferings and the dangers of people everywhere. One day, an elderly woman had the opportunity to explain to the Pope that her deceased husband had been defrauded of his editorial rights by a Vatican executive. She had no income to raise her family. After listening to her story and verifying the incident, the Pope wished to make amends. The widow was awarded 2,000,000 lire.

Sister Domenica accompanied her kindergarten class to the Vatican for a papal audience. As Pius XII was passing near her group, she lifted a little girl toward the Pope and asked him to read a letter the child brought from her mother. As the Pope was leaving the audience, he walked directly to this group and whispered to Sister Domenica: "Tell me, what is the nature of the letter?" Sister explained that the child's mother had to go to the hospital for a serious operation but did not have money. The Holy Father looked at the child, blessed her, and said, "I'll take care of the matter." The following day a letter arrived with a personal check from

Pius XII for 30,000 lire, which was more than enough for the operation.

In 1954, Pius XII became gravely ill and considered abdication of his office. Only when the doctors assured him that he would recover and would soon be able to resume his duties, did he resign himself to remain as Pope. In fact, he continued his mission and gave four more years of fruitful service to the Church.

During his final illness, when he could no longer celebrate Holy Mass, Pius XII repeated constantly the *Anima Christi*. When he died, the saintly Padre Pio—one of the most charismatic figures of the twentieth-century (beatified May 2, 1999 and canonized June 16, 2002)—was consoled "by a vision of the former pontiff in his heavenly home" (*Diario*, p. 225). On May 26, 2002, Elena Rossignani Pacelli confirmed this statement. With her mother, the Pope's sister Elisabetta, she visited Padre Pio who spoke about this vision. Referring to Pius XII's sanctity in his letter to Margherita Marchione (February 22, 2001), Bernard Tiffany quoted the following letter from Padre Pio's secretary, Reverend Dominic Meyer, OFM, Cap.: "Padre Pio told me he saw the Pope in Heaven during his Mass. Many miracles have been attrributed to the Pope's intercession in various parts of the world (June 30, 1959)."

The Servant of God, Edvige Carboni, a contemporary of Padre Pio da Pietrelcina, lived in Rome during the entire pontificate of Pope Pius XII. Throughout her correspondence she repeated certain expressions about the Pope: "Our Pope is truly a saint!" "During the war we suffered so much! If it had not been for the help of the Holy Father, we would have all died of hunger." "Those were difficult times, but the Holy Father, the Pope, came to us and to all Rome with help, giving us bread. And also clothing. Our Pope is a saint! Love him."

Although he was ill, on September 30, 1958, the Holy Father received the children from Villa Nazareth for their annual audience. He did not want to diasppoint the children. He remained with them for half an hour, aways serene, tranquil and smiling. As they approached him individually, he distributed candy to each child.

In a conversation with me, Father Antonio Furioli recalled the emotion experienced when Pius XII died on October 9, 1958. Everyone in his family loved him. Antonio was very young and cried with his mother and family. He stated: "Everyone was sad. For days my mother kept a candle lighted before an image of Pius XII and together we prayed and shed tears. It was a spontaneous and sincere tribute toward someone we felt was a family friend. I remember that I was inconsolable. This was my first experience with death. The first great sorrow of my life. Pius XII remained a model that inspired me to become a priest."

## *Prayerful Spirit*

Prayers written by His Holiness penetrate the mystery of God and contain the quiet acknowledgment of the Divine Presence. They capture the richness, the depth, or the majesty of God. They are a work of love that weaves its way into the mysterious realm of the spirit. In them one truly finds spiritual strength.

As a tribute of love for the fifteenth anniversary of his coronation, some of his prayers were published by the Pontificia Opera di Assistenza; others were found in the *Acta Apostolicae Sedis*. In 1956, Newman Press included many of them in an English translation by Reverend Martin Schoenberg, OSC.

These prayers also reveal Pius XII's special devotion to Saints Dominic; Catherine, the Lily of Virginity; Thérèse of the Child Jesus; Pius X; North American Martyrs. Among them is one to Maria Goretti who is a model for all young people. Soon after she received her First Holy Communion, a young man killed her when she refused to commit sin. Pius XII canonized her. The Pope's "Prayer to Maria Goretti" acknowledges her fidelity to the Divine Spouse: "In you, may childhood and youth find refuge, so that they may be protected from every contamination, and be enabled to walk the paths of life with the serenity and the joy of the pure of heart. Amen."

Prayers written by the Vicar of Christ inspired the faithful. They are prayers of a deeply religious person, a Shepherd of Souls, keenly aware of the problems, interests, and cares of his flock. Their depth, beauty, and forceful expression will prompt the individual to meditate. Prayers to Jesus are entitled: The Crucified Saviour; The Redeemer; The Risen Saviour; The Eternal Wisdom; The Divine Teacher; The King of Ages; The Prince of Peace.

Pope Pius XII constantly and prayerfully raised his thoughts to God. He requested prayers for the month of May. He referred to a world "poisoned by lies and disloyalty and wounded by excesses of violence," as he condemned the invasions of Belgium, Holland, and Luxemburg (May 11, 1940). He wrote prayers for different occasions: A Prayer for Peace; Children's Prayer for Peace; Prayer to the Holy Spirit for the Church. He wrote prayers for: The Cessation of War; Victims of War; The Suffering; The Sick. There are numerous other prayers: Prayer for Youth; Scouts; Women; Jurists; Religious Vocations; Priestly Holiness.

When the Pope announced the Holy Year of 1950, he spoke of the part religion and faith were to play in celebrating it. He decreed that the benefits of the Jubilee could be granted "to those who cannot see, to the sick, the poor, to those in prison and to the faithful of both sexes in those countries in which on account of particular circumstances they are not allowed to undertake the pilgrimage to Rome." This was an important innovation. For the occasion he wrote "The Holy Year Prayer" which includes these words: "... Grant, O Lord, peace in our days—peace to souls, peace to families, peace to our country, peace among nations. May the rainbow of peace cover with the sweep of its serene light the land sanctified by the life and passion of Thy Divine Son...."

It is interesting to note that the telegrams sent to the King of Belgium, the Queen of Holland, and the Grand Duchess of Luxemburg were prepared directly by Pius XII. The day before he had ordered the preparation of a protest against the Nazi invasions. Cardinal Maglione had personally written a brief note to be published that very evening in *L'Osservatore Romano*. When His Holinesss read it, it seemed too weak. Others, too, had prepared a draft for the Pope and sent it to the Secretary of State. This would be ready at 8 p.m. In the meantime, the Pope prayed and then he himself composed the three telegrams. Without delay, these letters were sent to the heads of Belgium, Holland, and Luxemburg that very day.

In the prayers written by Pius XII, besides sentiments of devotion, one finds doctrinal and moral statements that illustrate his profound thoughts and considerations. For example, the duties of a Christian spouse and mother are contained in the *Prayer of a Christian Woman to Mary, Our Most Holy Queen*: "Make us pure and fearless in our sentiments and in our actions; toward our loving, affectionate, and understanding spouse, make us affectionate companions; toward our children, make us diligent, vigilant, wise mothers; make us careful administrators of our domestic hearth; exemplary citizens of our beloved country; faithful daughters of the Church, ever ready to be guided by her in thought and action." (*Discorsi*, Vol. XX, p. 542.)

Professional morality for doctors to follow is integrated in *A Doctor's Prayer*: "Imitating your example, make us paternal in our compassion, sincere in our advice, diligent in our care for patients, solicitous in avoiding deception, delicate in announcing the mystery of pain and of death; above all, may we be firm in defending your holy law of respect for life, against the assaults of egoism and perverse instincts." (*Discorsi*, Vol. XIX, p. 892.)

The obligations of Christian politicians are summarized in the *Prayer of Catholic Representatives and other Political Officials*: "Eternal and majestic God, Creator and Lord of all things, Supreme Legislator and Ruler...we implore your help in this office that we intend to accept and exercise for the greater spiritual and material good of our people.

"Grant us an understanding of our duties that will guide us in the preparation and implementation of our efforts, united with objectivity and healthy realism, to lead us and perceive clearly that which in each moment seems to be the best approach. Do not make us depart from that healthy impartiality, toward which we must strive, without unjust preferences for the good of all. Never allow us to be lacking in loyalty toward our people, but to have faith in the principles that we openly profess and to have the loftiness of spirit to keep us above all possible corruption or personal interests.

"Make our deliberations serene, without passion other than that inspired by a holy desire of truth; that our resolutions be in conformity with your precepts, even if your will should impose on us sorrow and renunciation; and that in our insignificance, we will strive to imitate that rectitude and sanctity with which you govern and direct us for the greater glory and true good of human society and of all your creatures" (*Discorsi,* Vol. XIX, p. 904).

Among Pope Pius XII's prayers honoring Our Lady are: The Immaculate Heart; Assumed into Heaven; Our Queen; Easter Prayer to Mary; Our Lady of Emigrants; Patroness of Catholic Action; Marian Year Prayer.

In preparation for the *Solemnity of the Assumption of Mary,* he expressed his deep love for the Madonna with this prayer:

*A great sign in the sky, a woman clothed with the sun, with the moon under her feet and on her head a crown of twelve stars.*

*Revelation 12:1*
**All:** *O Immaculate Virgin, Mother of God and Mother of all peoples.*

**Leader:** *We believe with all the fervor of our faith in your triumphal assumption, both in body and soul, into heaven, where you are acclaimed as Queen by all the choirs of angels and the whole company of heaven.*

**All:** *And we unite with them to praise and bless the Lord who has exalted you above all other pure creatures, and to offer you the tribute of our devotion and love.*

**Leader:** *We know that your gaze, which on earth watched over the humble and suffering humanity of Jesus, in heaven is filled with the vision of that humanity glorified, and with the vision of uncreated wisdom, and that the joy of your soul in the direct contemplation of the adorable Trinity causes your heart to throb with overwhelming tenderness.*

**All:** *And we, poor sinners, whose body weighs down the flight of the soul, beg you to purify our hearts so that, while we remain here below we may learn to see God and God alone in the beauties of his creatures.*

**Leader:** *We trust that your merciful eyes may deign to glance down upon our miseries and our sorrows; upon our struggles and our weaknesses; that your countenance may smile upon our joys and our victories; that you may hear the voice of Jesus saying to you of each one of us, as he once said to you of his beloved disciple: Behold your son.*

**All:** *And we, who call upon you as our Mother, we, like John, take you as the guide, strength, and consolation of our mortal life.*

**Leader:** *We are inspired by the certainty that your eyes, which wept over the earth watered by the blood of Jesus, are yet turned toward this world, held in the clutch of wars, persecutions, oppression of the just and the weak.*

**All:** *And from the shadows of this vale of tears, we seek in your heavenly assistance and tender mercy comfort for our aching hearts and help in the trials of the Church, and of our fatherland.*

**Leader:** *We believe, finally, that in the glory where you reign, clothed with the sun and crowned with the stars, you are, after Jesus, the joy and gladness of all the angels and of all the saints.*

**All:** *And from this earth, over which we tread as pilgrims, comforted by our faith in future resurrection, we look to you, our life, our sweetness and our hope. Draw us onward with the sweetness of your voice that one day, after our exile, you may show us Jesus, the blessed fruit of your womb, O clement, O loving, O sweet Virgin Mary.*

*Pius pp. XII*

Pope Pius XII wrote a prayer for the feast of the Nativity of Mary:

*Enraptured by the splendor of your heavenly beauty, and impelled by the anxieties of the world, we cast ourselves into your arms, O Immaculate Mother of Jesus and our Mother, Mary, confident of finding in your most loving heart appeasement of our ardent desires, and a safe harbor from the tempests which beset us on every side.*

*Though degraded by our faults and overwhelmed by infinite misery, we admire and praise the peerless richness of sublime gifts with which God has filled you, above every other mere creature, from the first moment of your conception until the day on which, after your assumption into heaven, he crowned you Queen of the Universe.*

*Crystal Fountain of faith, bathe our minds with the eternal truths! O fragrant Lily of all holiness, captivate our hearts with your heavenly perfume! O Conqueress of evil and death, inspire in us a deep horror of sin which makes the soul detestable to God and a slave of hell! O well-beloved of God, hear the ardent cry which rises up from every heart.*

*Bend tenderly over our aching wounds. Convert the wicked, dry the tears of the afflicted and oppressed, comfort the poor and humble, quench hatreds, sweeten harshness, safeguard the flower of purity in youth, protect the holy Church, make all peoples feel the attraction of Christian goodness.*

*In your name, resounding harmoniously in heaven, may they recognize that they are brothers and sisters, and that the nations are members of one family, upon which may there shine forth the sun of a universal and sincere peace. Receive, O most sweet Mother, our humble supplications, and above all obtain for us that we may one day repeat before your throne that hymn which today is sung on earth around your altars: You are all beautiful, O Mary! You are the glory, you are the joy, you are the honor of our people.*

*Pius pp. XII*

Pius XII's spirituality can be traced to his profound religious family upbringing and to the education he received in preparation for his ministry. As a priest and throughout his life he kept by his bedside a book by a 19th century French spiritual writer by the name of Jacques-Benigne Bossuet, an eloquent orator, whose literary style was admired by Pius XII; an intellectual, a master of French Catholic thought whose emphasis was on the immutability of doctrine and the perfection of God's Church. His writings helped avoid a schism between the French King and the Pope.

Indeed, Bossuet's writings influenced Eugenio Pacelli, who was inspired by this author's ideal of the priesthood, his respect for St. Vincent de Paul's charitable works, his love for the poor in the Church.

Bossuet's orations display dignity and balance, thematic development, as well as emotional passages logically organized. He appealed directly to the heart of individuals as he selected qualities and episodes which enabled them to draw a moral conclusion. In clear, simple rhetoric he convinced his listeners by the passion of his religious feelings and convictions.

Interested in the unity of the Church, Bossuet was involved in the Gallican controversy, as well as in the issues of Jansenism and Quietism. His sermons included not only religious but also political matters. Abounding in biblical citations and paraphrases, they displayed moderation, opposed the persecution of innocent people, and defended the Church Fathers and the Catholic traditions.

Bossuet's influence may be found in Pope Pius XII's discourses and other writings. It may be assumed, therefore, that Pius XII read passages from the book at his bedside before retiring.

No doubt, too, Pacelli's prayer life sustained his faith, nourished his hope and made more fruitful his charity. When Cardinal Tardini recited the *Magnificat* in his eulogy at Pius XII's funeral, he was asked why that particular prayer. He answered: "Because the *Magnificat* is the canticle of humility and, in all my life, I have never met a more humble person than Eugenio Pacelli."

*Pius XII pleaded for the safety of "those ex-
pelled from their native land and deported to
foreign lands." (December 24, 1941)*

# Part III: Papal Audiences

Even before "official" audiences, thousands were able
to greet Eugenio Pacelli when he represented the papacy in
various parts of the world. In 1936, he arrived in the New
York harbor on the *Conte di Savoia*. The Vatican Secretary
of State traveled in the United States aboard a United Air-
lines DC-3 chartered plane, from Roosevelt Field, Long Island. This "unofficial" trip covered some eight thousand
miles in seven days over congested cities, rocky mountains
and flat lands.

Captain Jack O'Brien was the pilot, and the stewardess
was Madeline Quirici, who spoke both English and Italian.
The Cardinal crisscrossed the United States addressing
thousands of American Catholics. He worked far into the
night inspiring the stewardess to say: "He was the most con-
siderate passenger I ever had. He was Christ-like." Pacelli
not only made an in-depth study of the American Church,
but he also appealed to the United States to throw open its
doors to Jewish refugees. His request went unheeded.

All who came to Pius XII's papal audiences were well
aware of his warmth. The overwhelming enthusiasm expressed during papal audiences reflects the universal esteem
for Pius XII and the belief that the Pope is, in fact, the representative of Christ on earth. He was always exhilarated by
the expressions of love and respect of servicemen and

women of every nation. One audience inspired American sailors to begin a rousing "Hip, hip, hooray—His Holiness!"

Each day, following Pius XII's meetings with Vatican staff members, he had private or general audiences. The Pope enjoyed receiving statesmen and workers; writers and artists; the young and the old; the sick and the suffering; religious and lay men and women. Offering their gifts, young people opened their hearts and confided to him their cherished dreams. As a father with his children, he spoke to them according to their particular state, profession, work or condition. He reminded them of their duties and obligations and had extraordinary insight into all types of problems.

Throughout his life Pacelli would find time for scholarly pursuits. In 1943, for example, in a discourse to the Pontifical Academy of Science, he forecast the development of atomic energy and discussed the disintegration which uranium undergoes when bombarded by neutrons. The Pope expressed the hope that its force would be harnessed for the service of man and not released for his destruction. In 1951 Pius XII spoke on modern science and the proofs for the existence of God. He addressed the International Astronomical Union and spoke on the histopathology of the central nervous system. His speeches ranged from international penal law, toleration, psychiatry and clinical psychology, to medical genetics, urology, ophthalmology, medico-moral problems, accountancy, economics, moral guidance, statistics. Most speeches were in French and Italian, but a few were in Spanish, German, English or Latin.

Screening for a general audience was not very intense. In fact, many ladies were not aware they had to dress according to protocol. One day, when asked to kneel, a young girl in culottes and wedgies and harlequin glasses refused. "I got a coat on—isn't that enough? I'm not a Catholic! Why

58

should I kneel?" Everyone was embarrassed. As the Pope arrived, the girl continued to abuse the guards. Suddenly the scene changed. The Pope approached her gently; she burst into tears on her knees. He comforted her and stretched forth his hands to raise her up, but she shook her head and begged his blessing. Pope Pius XII blessed her.

Pius XII's love was manifested by his compassion. With thousands of people in larger audiences, the Pope had to move swiftly. One day, there was a woman with a blind baby. He spoke consoling words to the woman while blessing her and the baby. After moving away, Pius XII hesitated, and then turned back. The Pope asked to hold the baby in his arms, pressed it tenderly to his heart, carefully protecting the child against his large, pectoral cross. He spoke quietly to the mother. The woman was weeping. So was Pius XII.

On one occasion, the chamberlain called a family of Americans who were waiting for an audience—father, mother and four children, the youngest in his mother's arms. When the baby began to cry, the mother pleaded with the chamberlain. He shook his head. The mother saw a young woman and ran toward her. "Will you hold my baby for me?" she asked, and the surprised woman took him in her arms. However, soon the mother came hurrying back. "Thank you," she said. "Let me have my baby. His Holiness says he doesn't care if he cries. He wants to see him!"

Buried in the large group of faithful during a general audience a soldier shifted uneasily on his crutches. He could not kneel. Suddenly he saw Pius XII's compassionate eyes looking at him. Walking toward him, the Pope extended his hand. The soldier fumbled his hat from his right hand to his left in order to grasp the Pope's, and he dropped it. His Holiness bent down, grabbed the hat, placed it in the soldier's trembling hand and embraced him. The young man suddenly relaxed and smiled. As the Pope moved on, the soldier leaned on his crutches, held his hat aloft in triumph, and then joined the crowd shouting, *Viva il Papa! Viva il Papa!*

During one papal audience, a group of American baseball players were amazed when Pius XII spoke about sports. One of them waited till the audience was almost over and, as the Pope turned away, he murmured, "I was a Cardinal once myself, Your Holiness." Immediately the Pope turned around: "And how could that have been, my son?" During the explanation, a perplexed Pius XII grinned. The baseball player treasures the Pope's reaction: "I guess I really walked into that one." Joe Medwick, of the Saint Louis Cardinals, could never figure out where he got the nerve to kid the Pope.

One day, an Anglican lady was invited to a private audience. She was alone and awaited the Pope in a small chamber. Now and then people dressed in the oddest fashions passed by: Swiss Guards wore an outfit designed by Michelangelo; others were in long robes. They reassured her that the Pope would soon arrive. When a tall, thin man wearing a white cassock arrived, he chatted with her. She responded to his gentle questioning and they had a few polite laughs. The Anglican lady whispered: "Confidentially, the main reason I want to see the Pope is because a lot of my Catholic friends gave me rosaries and medals and Lord knows what else for him to bless." "We shall be happy to do so," said the man in white. The lady's jaw dropped. "Oh, no," she gulped. "You're the Pope!"

In 1950, the Pope welcomed Olsen and Johnson. "Laughter has no religion," Pius XII wistfully emphasized, as he spoke about God's generosity with the gift of laughter. "There should be more of it in the world." A few days after the liberation of Rome, Lieutenant General Mark Clark, Commander of the Fifth Allied Army, paid his respects to the Pope: "I am afraid you have been disturbed by the noise of my tanks. I am sorry." Pius XII smiled and replied: "General, any time you come to liberate Rome, you can make just as much noise as you like."

Robert Murphy, U.S. Undersecretary of State, and Pius XII were among the diplomats in Germany during the mid-1920s. When they met after the war, Murphy reminisced about how they had underestimated Hitler. Both had reported to their governments that he would never come to power. In response to Murphy, the Pope smiled and said, "In those days, you see, I was not infallible."

Leo Longanesi—a renowned Italian journalist and publisher—was indignant over the anticlerical campaigns against the Church. One day he suggested to the Pope that a particular day be designated when all Italian newspapers in Italy would print the full story about the charitable works of the Church during World War II. Pius XII responded: "Only God must be testimony to what is done for our neighbor!"

Although Pius XII would not publicize his own good deeds, others have. An example of his actions on behalf of Jewish refugees appeared in the *International Herald Tribune* (October 22, 2001). This story is part of the official Italian war record. Leonardo Marinelli was a commander in the Royal Finance Guard in the Aprica internment camp in northern Italy from 1943 to 1945.

An entry in his *Diary* records that on September 12, 1943, the Pope sent Giuseppe Carozzi, a young Italian priest to Marinelli requesting that 300 Jewish Yugoslav internees be given permits to Switzerland. Despite strict Nazi orders forbidding Jews, prisoners of war, or anyone who had not joined Mussolini's northern Italian puppet Republic of Salò from crossing the border, Marinelli complied with the Pope's wishes. During the next four days as the group crossed the border, guards were seen "carrying bags for some of the fugitives." Later, Marinelli himself was placed in an internment camp by the Nazis. He escaped. In his testimony to the Finance Guard High Command in July 1945, Marinelli confirmed what he had written in his *Diary*.

The Pope enjoyed receiving people of every nation and rank, including statesmen and laborers; writers and artists; the young and the old; the sick and the suffering; religious and laity. Offering their gifts, young people opened their hearts and confided to him their cherished dreams. As a father with his children, he spoke to them according to their particular state, profession, work or condition. The enthusiasm during general audiences for people in all walks of life was electrifying!

One day a woman knelt to kiss Pius XII's ring, and it remained in her hand. He was not aware that his ring had slipped off his hand. The elderly woman screamed that she had to see the Pope. The guards wanted to arrest her, but the Pope smilingly told her to approach him and then asked her to slip back on his finger the Fisherman's ring.

Another incident was not so pleasant. When the Holy Father gave his hand to one visitor, the man slid the ring from his finger. Only when a chamberlain whispered, "Your ring, Holiness!" did he turn back and, standing in front of the thief, say, "I think my ring slipped from my finger." The man was trembling as he opened his hand. The Pope gently took the ring and walked away.

Each day a bus from a Minor Seminary in Rome arrived at Saint Peter's Basilica bringing young boys wearing red cassocks and white surplices to serve the private Masses of visiting priests from all parts of the world. They were entrusted with a special kit with unconsecrated hosts and wine. Between Masses they would walk in and out of rooms to see if their services were needed. One day two fourteen-year-old seminarians were in this group.

Having made a wrong turn, they were in a labyrinth of halls and beautifully decorated rooms. At that early hour they did not encounter many people. Those who passed by, smiled, but did not question them. After all, they were dressed as altar boys and everyone assumed they knew where to go. They roamed around in a leisurely manner, not only intrigued but truly fascinated by the splendor.

However, the young seminarians were frightened when they realized they were lost. They panicked as they rushed in and out of rooms and corridors. Finally they reached a small library. As they entered, a kind-looking priest in a white cassock asked if he could help them. They explained they were lost. Taking them by the hand, he told them not to worry. He invited them to a room in an adjoining apartment where he served them cookies and milk. While the boys enjoyed the treat, the priest spoke to them in a friendly manner. He then said: "Now the Holy Father gives you and your family a special blessing." The boys, shocked to learn they were with the Pope, knelt down for the blessing.

As they chatted, the Pope then directed them to Saint Peter's Square. He advised them to go to the bus. Thrilled with this extraordinary experience, the boys, upon returning to the Seminary, related every detail of their encounter with the Pope. The altar boys had been lost, but they found His Holiness, Pope Pius XII. One of the boys later became a priest. His name is Father Joseph Rinaldo.

Pius XII was a minister of peace in a warring world. When he was told that Stalin inquired about the number of divisions in his army, he said: "You may tell my son Joseph he will meet my divisions in heaven." That was Pacelli's secret. Even of Stalin he could say "my son." And mean it. He spoke many languages, but the only language that inspired others, was the language of his heart.

Pius XII enjoyed telling the story that one day he asked a toddler in Castelgandolfo how old she was. The little girl answered: "I don't know!" He repeated his question. She confirmed her response: "I don't know! Dad says one thing and mamma says another." When His Holiness asked her if she went to school, the young student answered very seriously: "Why, yes, I attend the kindergarten of the older children!"

Pius XII was a modern Pope, working for peace and freedom for all. His service to the Church was a labor of love, inspired by the words of Saint Augustine: "Where there is love, there is no labor, and if labor there be, the labor itself is love!" Pius XII's words of wisdom also reflect Saint Augustine: "We come from you, O Lord, and our hearts are restless until they return to you for all eternity."

It was obvious that His Holiness Pope Pius XII considered the world his family. The Vatican was open to all the persecuted: Catholics, Protestants, Jews, and unbelievers. He encouraged progress in science, giving his blessing to the conquest of space in order that the human spirit might "understand ever more profoundly the infinite greatness of the Creator."

During the audiences he greeted his guests with a smile in his eyes and spoke to each one as a friend. Always a gentleman, he tried to save people from embarrassment. One American congressman asked him to bless a package of medals. He accidentally pulled out of his pocket a pack of cigarettes. The Pope blessed it. As he put it back in his pocket, the congressman blushed with embarrassment, but the Pope laughed and then blessed the medals.

A friendly human being, Pius XII never lost his dignity as the Vicar of Christ. He modeled his life on that of Jesus,

*Young girls from different parts of the world present gifts to the Holy Father on his birthday.*

*Three young boys carrying flowers were met by a smiling Pope as he walked in his garden.*

*Pope Pius XII praying
before the Crucifix.*

*Pope Pius XII
prays for peace.*

*Pope Pius XII
enjoys his visitors
during a General
Audience.*

*Monument erected in San Lorenzo Square on July 19, 1967.*

*(La Domenica del Corriere) After the devastation of the Basilica of San Lorenzo during the bombing of Rome, the Holy Father blessed the people and distributed funds to the needy.*

*(La Domenica degli Italiani) Over 50,000 children surround the Pope in the Basilica of St. Peter.*

*(La Tribuna Illustrata) The Pope is depicted in St. Peter's Square during the Holy Year procession on the feast of* Corpus Domini.

*Holy Father at his desk uses the typewriter.*

*Pope Pius XII caresses the lambs in his garden at Castelgandolfo.*

*Pope Pius XII blesses the world.*

*Mosaic depicting Pius XII praying in the National Shrine of the Immaculate Conception in Washington, D.C.*

*Pope Pius XII.*

*A smiling Holy Father greets his people from the Sedia Gestatoria.*

*A child presents flowers on the Pope's birthday.*

the Teacher. People of all races, religions, and professions spoke freely to him.

One day, Pius XII learned that a woman and her extremely deformed son had arrived in Rome and were refused an audience. He immediately ordered a car to be sent to the mother and child. When they arrived, he took the boy in his arms and asked the mother what had been done for him. "I took him to Lourdes because doctors could do nothing. There was no miracle, but my son wanted to see you. We want the assurance that God is with us." The Pope warmly gave her that faith, as he comforted them blessing her and the boy in his arms.

During an audience, one ambassador mentioned having noticed a mountain piper waiting. Interrupting their discussion, the Pope and the ambassador approached the piper and asked him to entertain them in the corridor.

All who came to the audiences were well aware of his warmth. Regardless of one's faith, people from all walks of life and of every religious denomination treasured a meeting with him. He reaffirmed the rights of the family, the rights of parents to supervise their children's education, and the rights of conscience, stressing the fundamental unity of all mankind under the fatherhood of God.

His appeals to the Allies are well known. It is an historical fact that when Rome was bombed, the Pope went to the Church of Saint Ignatius Loyola and prayed before the image of the *Madonna del Divino Amore*. Both clergy and faithful of Rome joined the Pontiff as he prayed for peace. The city of Rome was saved from total destruction!

Pope Pius XII's saintly life and heroic virtues have also been recorded. He was prophetic in his 1942 Christmas message outlining the basic elements of Judeo-Christian civilization and warning the world not to violate them. He condemned the murder of hundreds of thousands of people marked down for death or progressive extinction. Indeed, evidence shows that the words and actions of the saintly Pope Pius XII can no longer be contested.

Among the most known Hungarian prelates is the Servant of God, Cardinal Jozsef Mindszenty who was imprisoned by both the Nazis and the Communists. He was tortured and, like Pius XII, defamed in order to destroy his reputation and that of the Catholic Church. During a Consistory in 1946, the Pope clearly stated: "You will be the first of the thirty-two new Cardinals who will endure martyrdom, symbolized by these purple robes!"

Their saintly rapport was underlined during the allocutions of Pius XII in 1948, when Cardinal Mindszenty was arrested and condemned and, in 1949, when the Hungarians fought the Soviet troops during their struggle for independence. The Cardinal was finally liberated in 1956. Expressing his love and gratitude toward his people, he showed them the two most precious items he possessed: a photograph of his mother and one of Pope Pius XII.

In the *Osservatore Romano* (March 30, 1939), Giuseppe De Luca wrote: "Pius XII's entire person bears the sign of interior discipline and control of his own soul. Patient, swift, courteous, meek and intransigent, he is the Pope of justice and peace. He is filled with the wisdom of God and of mankind; he is the joy and hope of those whom he leads; he attracts strangers to his kingdom—those who believe and those who do not believe whom he addressed in his first message with unspeakable sweetness."

Years later, in another article (*Profughi,* Spring, 1945), De Luca wrote: "Looking back to the past sorrowful years, and to the desolation experienced in Rome, one must say that Pope Pius XII, no one but the Pope, saved Rome from complete destruction... ."

*"He who makes a distinction between Jews and other men is unfaithful to God and is in conflict with God's commands." (June 2, 1943)*

# Part IV: A Saintly Life

Pope Pius XII led the papacy in a ceaseless search for peace. He spread a culture of peace, and enriched the lives of others by constructing a more just and peaceful society.

When Eugenio Pacelli was Vatican Secretary of State, he denounced Nazism as well as anti-Semitism and demonstrated concern for persecuted Jews and other refugees. As Pope, he not only issued orders to protect them, but also provided money and supplies for their maintenance. On the eve of World War II, the international position of the Vatican was dangerous and difficult.

The historic evidence during Pope Pius XII's pontificate testifies to his sanctity, courage and integrity, as well as to his efforts to prevent the war and to shelter countless victims of the Nazis. The anti-Semitic decrees enacted by Mussolini in 1938 were causing bitter conflicts between Italy and the Holy See.

In view of the plight of the Jewish people of Europe, resolutions were adopted at the January 1939 meeting of the Jewish Congress in Geneva. Dr. Nahum Goldmann, chairman, stated: "We record the Jewish people's deep appreciation of the stand taken by the Vatican against the advance of resurgent paganism which challenges all traditional values of religion as well as inalienable human rights upon which alone enduring civilization can be found."

As a diplomat, Pius XII saw war approaching and instructed the papal representatives to Germany, Italy, France, Poland and England to learn whether mediation by the Pope would be considered. On August 24, 1939 he gave each papal representative the text of a speech asking them to convey it to their respective governments. That evening he read the speech to the world: "The danger is imminent, but there is still time. Nothing is lost with peace; all can be lost with war."

On September 1, 1939, Nazi tanks crossed the Polish border. This was the beginning of World War II. In his encyclical, *Summi Pontificatus* (October 27, 1939), Pius XII condemned Hitler's actions. On December 28, 1939, the Pope paid a ceremonial call on King Victor Emmanuel III and Queen Elena at the Quirinal Palace. The visit was to return that made by the King and Queen a week earlier, and also to demonstrate the Vatican's support of Italy's neutrality.

Without interruption before and during World War II, Pius XII continued his work for peace, striving to heal the wounds inflicted by this great tragedy. The papacy rescued Jews by channeling money to those in need, issuing countless baptismal certificates for their protection, negotiating with Latin American countries to grant them visas, and keeping in touch with their relatives through the Vatican Information Service.

During the North African campaign a boatload of Allied wounded arrived in Italy for hospitalization and imprisonment. A Vatican representative boarded the boat and distributed forms among the soldiers who immediately filled, signed and addressed them. Within weeks after their capture the families of these American soldiers received information sent airmail by the Vatican to the United States.

68

A wounded son of an Episcopalian family in Washington, DC, was listed as "missing" by the War Department because the Nazis had failed to report him to the International Red Cross as having been captured. The soldier was convalescing in a hospital in Italy. A Vatican official found him and notified his parents.

Communicating with the families of prisoners of war, the Vatican described details of injuries, deaths, internment, and photographs of the resting-place or turned over to the office of the American *chargé d'affaires* the belongings of soldiers. This was a sad, yet consoling work of mercy. As an expression of gratitude for news that their son was a war prisoner and not dead, a Baptist family in Kansas, sent the Holy Father their weekly tithe of twenty-two dollars.

As president of the university student group of Catholic Action, Giulio Andreotti was closely associated with the Vatican. He met frequently with Pius XII who was interested in student life and cultural formation and in obtaining the opinions of university students. In his book, *A ogni morte di Papa* (Rizzoli, 1980), Andreotti writes that Pius XII possessed exceptional gentleness.

One day the young student experienced a forty-five minute delay for his private audience. As soon as Pope Pius XII arrived, he went directly to Andreotti to excuse himself. He explained that a group of soldiers requested to meet with him before their departure for the front lines and he could not refuse to see them.

Pius XII was particularly interested in university students who were on the battlefield, anxious to know if they kept in touch with their professors and chaplains and if they were visiting the poor according to the directives of Saint Vincent de Paul. When the student newspaper, *Azione Fucina,* was suspended for one month, the Pope sent a diplomatic protest to the civil authorities. During a papal audience, Andreotti asked the Holy Father to read a letter from a soldier who was unable to receive Holy Communion because he could not observe the requirement for fasting. Immediately, Pius XII instructed him to request special consideration for the soldier and for all other similar cases.

Andreotti also recalls sending a note to the Pope asking him to refrain from speaking about "Catholic Communists" for fear of endangering the lives of students who were in prison. Following his advice, the Pope substituted that talk with a splendid discourse addressing the Fascists who were spreading falsehoods, saying that the Pope was in favor of war, etc. A few days later, Pius XII placed his hand on Andreotti's shoulder and asked, "Was it ok?" No one, except the young university student, understood the meaning of that statement.

In his discourse of September 7, 1947 to members of the "Men of Catholic Action," after declaring that he had always served the cause of peace, the Pope explained in detail the meaning of serving the cause of peace.: "To the intercession of the Mother of God and of the Saints, We confide that good, to which all of you, the entire Italian population and the great family of nations, ardently yearns for: *Peace*; not the peace that is only apparent and legal, but the peace that is real and just. We ourselves—regardless of how the enemies of the Papacy, to whom We send Our love and Our best wishes, misrepresent Our intentions and Our words—We ourselves have always served and will continue to serve the cause of true peace, until Our last breath. You, too, Men of Catholic Action, must become champions of this holy cause. To serve peace is to serve justice. To serve peace is to serve the good of the people, especially the humble and the deprived. To serve peace is to look toward the future with a firm and steady eye. To serve peace is to hasten the day in which all peoples, without exception, having stopped rivalry and disputes, will unite in a fraternal embrace. To serve peace is to save civilization. To serve peace is to preserve the human family from unutterable new misfortunes. To serve peace is to elevate one's spirit toward heaven and away from the domination of Satan. To serve peace is to fulfill the sovereign law of God, which is the law of goodness and of love." (*Discorsi*, Vol. IX, p. 220.)

Documents confirm that Pius XII was indeed a champion of peace, freedom, human dignity; a pastor who encouraged Catholics to look on Christians and Jews as their brothers and sisters in Christ, all children of a common Father. He was a witness of love, and the Servant of the servants of God.

With the opening of the Vatican Archives, the prejudice and insensitivity of some scholars should cease. New evidence has emerged and will vindicate this wartime Pontiff. Documents on pre-war Vatican-German relations will counter the criticism by some scholars. In a letter dated April 13, 1938, when Cardinal Pacelli was Secretary of State (1929-1939), Pope Pius XI ordered the rectors and presidents of Catholic universities worldwide, to refute each and every one of Nazism's racist theories. The text of the letter signed by the secretary of the Sacred Congregation for Seminaries and Universities (now the Congregation for Catholic Education) was published in the monthly *Nouvelle Revue Théologique*, 1939, Volume 66.

A respected British scholar, Sir Martin Gilbert, praised Pius XII's efforts throughout World War II on behalf of the Jews. He defended Pius XII in his book, *The Righteous* (2003), stating that the Pope's 1942 Christmas message condemning racism was viewed by the Nazis as a defense of the persecuted Jews. In July 2000, another Jewish historian, Richard Breitman, revealed that "Hitler distrusted the Holy See because it hid Jews." Rabbi David Dalin declared that "Daniel Jonah Goldhagen's polemic against Pius XII, John Paul II, and the Catholic Church fails to meet even the minimum standards of scholarship."

In a world of unprecedented evil and violence, Pius XII made every effort to alleviate human suffering caused by the Second World War. He laid the foundations for the great insights of the Second Vatican Council. His spirituality and theological vision, his compassionate commitment to the poor, the sick and the victims of Nazism, Fascism and Communism, cannot be ignored.

Pius XII was not silent. He made every effort to help Jews and other victims of the Nazis through quiet diplomacy. It suffices to check the *New York Times* where his words indicate clearly that he was defending the Jews and other refugees.

In the cities of Livorno, Lucca and Pisa, over 800 Jews were saved from Nazi persecution in 1943-44, thanks to Pius XII's appeal. The testimony of Giorgio Nissim, a Jew from Pisa, who died in 1976, confirms that Pius XII ordered the network of Catholic assistance in Tuscany to maintain relations with the Jewish movement, "Delasem."

Nissim's children found documents that include Gino Bartali, one of the greatest cyclists in Italian history, who also collaborated in the initiative. To save refugees, Bartali hid false documents in the crossbar of his bicycle. Recently, his son Andrea explained his father's participation: "His task was to take the photos and papers to clandestine printers to produce the false documents. One day the Fascists cornered him and advised him not to go near any Catholic institutions. He told them he would do what he wanted. However, he returned home and said, 'Children, we are going to hide in a little town near Arezzo.' The family left. He did not go. He remained with Nissim and continued his work to save others (*Corriere della Sera*, April 3, 2003)."

Representing the Hebrew Commission, Dr. Joseph Nathan, addressed the Jewish community at the end of World War II. He expressed gratitude to those who protected and saved Jews during the Nazi-Fascist persecutions. "Above all," he stated, "we acknowledge the Supreme Pontiff and the religious men and women who, executing the directives of the Holy Father, recognized the persecuted as their brothers and, with great abnegation, hastened to help them, disregarding the terrible dangers to which they were exposed."

Vatican relief efforts—clothes, food, medicine, books—for the suffering throughout the world stemmed from Pius XII. Countless cases of food, clothing, medicine, and other necessities were distributed by the Vatican to all the needy. The farm at Castelgandolfo supplied much of the produce, eggs, cheese, and milk to Vatican City residents who could buy at its supermarket at one-half the cost elsewhere. During World War II there were four hundred New Hampshire chickens for eggs, and nearly fifty Frisian cows for milk. Much of what the farm provided was sent free to a hospital in Rome.

Pius XII took care of his flock and remained in Rome during the war to assist them. When Jews and other refugees were hidden in the Vatican, the Pope provided for their needs. He gave orders that, whenever possible, Kosher foods for the Jews were to be supplied. Because everyone else could not have heat during the winter months, he refused to have heat in his apartment. He would not accept coffee during the war when he could not serve it to his "guests."

In 1943, as millions of Jews and other Europeans suffered the horrors of the Holocaust, the Allies bombed the eternal city during a two-hour attack. The Holy Father hurried from the Vatican to the streets of Rome. He stood in the midst of terrorized people as buildings collapsed in piles of smoldering rubble and bombs exploded on all sides. The Romans ran toward him for guidance and strength. With hands and white cassock smeared with the blood of the dead and the wounded, Pius XII blessed and consoled his flock. While civil authorities fled, the Pontiff personally took care of the immediate needs of the victims, providing food and distributing funds to the homeless. This scene is portrayed by the artist Achille Beltrame in *La Domenica del Corriere*, August 1, 1943, with the caption: "After the destruction of the Basilica of San Lorenzo during the bombing of Rome, the Holy Father blessed the people and distributed funds to the needy."

Pius XII's voice was heard around the world. It was the "Voice" of a tireless world leader whose contribution to humanity during the Holocaust is incontrovertible. Rabbi Marc Saperstein wrote in *The Washington Post*, April 1, 1998: "The fundamental responsibility for the Holocaust lies with the Nazi perpetrators. Not with Pope Pius XII. Not with the Church. Not with the teachings of the Christian faith."

Pope Pius XII was a man of compassionate commitment to the poor, the sick, and especially those who were the victims of Nazi and other ideological perversities of the twentieth century, such as Fascism and Communism. He was a man of vision.

With both Allies and Nazis, Pius XII insisted that Rome be spared. On June 4, 1944, the Nazis evacuated the Eternal City in an orderly fashion. Amidst tears and acclamations, crowds gathered in Saint Peter's Square throughout the day to thank the Holy Father for saving Rome from destruction.

The noted writer, Aldo Palazzeschi, recalled how, when civil authorities disappeared, the moral figure of the Pope became the leader of Rome: "…The Romans knew that there was a person who protected them and no earthly force would be capable of removing him. When the war broke out, after having advised, exhorted, and implored leaders, after having made his paternal and saddened voice heard in the name of humanity threatened by the terrible scourge of war, the Vicar of Christ as head of Christianity took upon his shoulders the Cross to Calvary. From that day, he sought every avenue, attempted every means to avoid, lessen, and alleviate the sorrows and sufferings of all." The Romans unanimously acclaimed Pope Pius XII, "*Defensor Civitatis.*"

During the years 1939-1955, Reverend Giacomo Martegani, former editor of the Jesuit magazine, *La Civiltà Cattolica*, was the director general of Vatican Radio. He was privileged to meet with the Servant of God, Pope Pius XII, every two weeks to discuss the many contemporary problems. He testified that "the high ideals and Christian virtues manifested by His Holiness, Pope Pius XII during these conversations were always an inspiration."

"I affirm that during my tenure as ambassador, people everywhere praised Pius XII's actions. I wish to join them in saying that he was a *prudent* Pope." These are the words of Gioachino Ruiz-Gimenez Cortes, International President of "Pax Romana" and Spanish Ambassador to the Holy See from 1948 to 1951.

Cortes testified to Pius XII's protection of the persecuted Jews during the Holocaust. Having participated in the preparations for the *Concordat* with Spain, Cortes maintains that he can attest to his personal sanctity and that "Pius XII was always animated by a priestly spirit." He also confirmed that others were of the same opinion: Archbishop Giovanni

Battista Montini, Attorney Vittorino Veronese, Professor of Philosophy Jorge del Vecchio who, when the Fascist government attacked all Jews, found refuge in the Vatican. Professor del Vecchio published several articles honoring Pius XII for all his accomplishments in favor of the victims of Nazism and Fascism.

Father Enrico Klein, SJ, was Director of Canisio College in Berlin. In 1946, he approached Pius XII and requested financial assistance to rebuild the College. On three different occasions, His Holiness sent funds for this purpose. Father Klein testified that he was impressed by this "absolutely priestly person, totally alien to contemporary politics. My conversations with Fathers Leiber, Heinrich and Gundlach confirmed my impressions about his virtuous life."

Monsignor Walter Adolph, former Vicar of the Diocese of Berlin, testified that Cardinals Bertram, Schulte, Faulhaber and Innitzer advised the Pope not to speak out. After the round-up in Holland, Cardinal Sapieha destroyed the thousands of leaflets sent by His Holiness to manifest his solidarity with the Polish people. The Cardinal did not circulate them for fear that more baptized Jews and Catholic Poles would be sent to the gas chambers. Monsignor Adolph observed that "Pius XII may have had a premonition of a crisis in the Church and tried to avoid secularization by his magisterium."

Count Enrico Galeazzi and Prince Carlo Pacelli, an attorney and the son of Pius XII's brother, Francesco, visited the Pope almost every evening to discuss Vatican affairs. They declared that "Pius XII practiced every virtue in an heroic manner, and already in his lifetime his sanctity was acclaimed."

As a Consultor for the Congregation of the Doctrine of the Faith, Reverend Guglielmo Hentrich, SJ, was a member of Pius XII's private secretariat. His statement on the life, activities and virtues of His Holiness are of primary importance. Pius XII's condemnation of the Nazi racial persecution is clear. As an impartial Head of State, he could not act differently.

His Eminence Cardinal Stefano Wyszynski, Primate of Poland, had many profound conversations with the Servant of God, Pope Pius XII. According to his testimony, the Pope was always priestly, spiritual and pastoral. The Pope listened to him with great attention, and "had great trust in the Polish Episcopate and did not want to interfere with their plans, their work and their actions. He spontaneously offered his help and continued to send financial and material assistance to Poland. Cardinal Wyszynski testified that "he is convinced that neither the Holy See, nor any international authority could have succeeded in stopping the Nazis' program of extermination of Jews." In his conversations, he was impressed and moved by the Pope's delicacy and understanding. He considered him an exceptional man whose eminent, virtuous qualities have been recognized.

Among the survivors of the Holocaust was Israel Zolli the Chief Rabbi of Rome. On July 14, 1944, *The American Hebrew* in New York published an interview with Rabbi Zolli. Having been hidden in the Vatican during the German occupation of Rome, he emphatically stated: "The Vatican has always helped the Jews and the Jews are very grateful for the charitable work of the Vatican, all done without distinction of race."

Rabbi Zolli was an eye-witness of the deportation of Rome's Jews by the Gestapo in 1943. After the war, he converted to Catholicism and, in gratitude to Pope Pius XII, took the baptismal name Eugenio. He later wrote his memoirs, *Before the Dawn* (1954). He devoted an entire chapter to the German occupation of Rome and praised the Pope's leadership: "...The Holy Father sent by hand a letter to the bishops instructing them to lift the enclosure from convents and monasteries."

In his book, *Antisemitismo*, Rabbi Zolli states: "World Jewry owes a great debt of gratitude to Pius XII for his repeated and pressing appeals for justice on behalf of the Jews and, when these did not prevail, for his strong protests against evil laws and procedures."

The person who can best attest to Pius XII's sanctity is Sister Pascalina Lehnert. She governed his household from 1923 to his death in 1958. With her testimony one gathers rich and detailed information on the spiritual life and activities of the Servant of God, whom she served faithfully and always respected his wishes. Sister Pascalina implemented the Pope's charitable works when he was Nuncio, Cardinal Secretary of State and Pontiff. He did not want his many good works and accomplishments revealed. He was a humble person.

"The Pope," wrote Sister Pascalina, "not only opened the doors of the Vatican to protect the persecuted, but he encouraged convents and monasteries to offer hospitality. The Vatican provided provisions for these people. The accusation that Pius XII was indifferent to the needs of the victims is without foundation. He ordered me to spend his inheritance and personal funds to provide for those who wished to leave Italy and go to Canada, Brazil or elsewhere. Note that $800 were needed for each person who emigrated. Many times the Pope would ask me to deliver a sealed envelope, containing $1,000 or more, to Jewish families." In general, while begging for help, the Jews who were in contact with Pope Pius XII insisted that he avoid any public action.

78

In her memoirs she explains that one day, Pius XII prepared an official protest to be published the following day in the *Osservatore Romano*. As he entered the kitchen and stood before the blazing fireplace, he told Sister Pascalina that he decided not to have his protest printed and would now burn it. She objected and reminded him that it might be useful in the future. Pius XII said: "This protest is stronger than that of the Dutch bishops. I thought about filing it but, if the Nazis come and find it, what will happen to the Catholics and Jews in Germany? No, it is better to destroy this strong protest." With that, he threw it into the fire. Instead, he ordered Amleto Cicognani, Apostolic Delegate in Washington, DC, to have the text of the Dutch bishops' protest published and circulated in the United States.

Sister Pascalina's testimony is among the hundreds of depositions for the beatification of Pius XII. She clearly stated that Pius XII did not issue a condemnation of Nazism because the German and Austrian bishops dissuaded him from making additional protests that would undoubtedly irritate Hitler. Jews and Christians had suffered in the past because of Vatican pronouncements and they feared increased retaliation.

In 1943, the Vatican learned that the Germans were planning to invade the Vatican and kidnap the Pope. Arrangements for a safe haven were developed by Attorney Milo di Villagrazia, Monsignor Edoardo Prettner Cippico and Count Enrico Galeazzi, Architect of the Apostolic Palaces. They met secretly with Sister Pascalina and agreed that the Pope would be clandestinely transferred to Galeazzi's villa, about 120 kilometers from the Vatican. From the villa, he would be accompanied to Spain, where General Francisco Franco Bahamonde would be honored to host him. Thus the Pope would be removed from the fury of the Nazis. When approached with this plan, Pius XII adamantly refused to leave the Vatican.

From 1939 to 1956, Reverend Riccardo Lombardi, SJ, had many private audiences with Pius XII, during which he discussed the need for a general reform of the Church and the means to fight Communism. With the Pope's approval, Father Lombardi founded the *Movement for a Better World.*

In October of 1938, Sister Maria Conrada Grabmair was sent to Rome and assigned as Cardinal Eugenio Pacelli's cook. She testified to his virtuous life and to the esteem in which he was held by all who knew him. They trusted him and asked for his blessing and prayers. She explained: "He was loved by people of all faiths. His doctor was Protestant, his dentist was Jewish. His charity was extended to all who sought his help."

Cardinal Giuseppe Siri, Archbishop of Genova, worked closely with Pius XII. With great precision Cardinal Siri testified and is firmly convinced about the sanctity of the Servant of God.

The spiritual director for Sister Maria Paola Zileri Dal Verme, a member of the Salesian Sisters of Zangberg, was Cardinal Eugenio Pacelli. He continued to direct her after becoming Pope. She describes how concerned he was during the war about the welfare of orphaned children; whenever possible he surrounded himself with them and increased their relief rations; on some occasions he had 50,000 children eating at the Vatican. She gives a detailed description of his virtues.

Dr. Guglielmo Sandfuchs, director of religious radio programs in Bavaria, is a biographer of the Servant of God. In this book, he claimed that people not only admired Pacelli as a great diplomat, but also revered him as a priest and shepherd of souls who was among the first to use modern technology in the Church. Dr. Sandfuchs states that the Pope possessed every virtue in a superior manner.

Bishop Simone Irschl states that, along with his diplomatic activities in Germany, Pacelli enjoyed many pastoral activities and had excellent rapport with his own staff and with the general public. Based on his personal observations, Bishop Irschl is convinced that the Servant of God practiced every virtue in a superior degree. Bishop Giuseppe Thalhmer notes that as Nunzio he was much loved by the entire population because of his gioviality, simplicity, and sincerity.

Cardinal Lorenzo Jager underlines the fact that the Pope cared for the poor, the refugees, the prisoners of war, and the Catholics living in areas occupied by the Russians. Thanks to his financial assistance, it was possible to construct 400 small churches. He notes also that assistance was extended to all refugees, regardless of political party or religion. Palmiro Togliatti, the head of the Communist party in Italy, was saved from arrest and deportation. During the 1948 elections, Togliatti defamed the Pope and the Church. When this was brought to Pius XII's attention, he responded that "one must not expect thanks when good is done toward another."

The Reverend Giovanni Waxenberger affirms that the Pope and Cardinal Faulhaber truly respected one another. He was impressed by the Pope's piety and devotion during sacred functions. For fifteen years Bishop Quirino Paganuzzi had personal contact with the Servant of God, and was the bearer of packages and messages to Bishops throughout Europe. Bishop Pietro Canisio Van Lierde provided details on the life and heroic virtues of the Servant of God. Dr. Curzio Hruska, the Pope's dentist, always considered him a saintly person.

Members of the Pacelli family, Prince Giulio and Marcantonio, who were his playmates and lived in the same apartment building in Rome, recalled the goodness and virtues of Eugenio Pacelli even as a child.

Cardinal Arcadio Maria Larraona was Prefect of the Sacred Congregation of Rites. He testified about the care given by the Pope to all matters concerning the Church and the attention given to Religious and Secular Institutes. Cardinal Antonio Samoré was Prefect of the Sacred Congregation of the Sacraments and met with the Pope every two days or, at least, weekly. He was convinced about the heroic virtues he possessed and the sanctity of his life. Reverend Angelo Martini, SJ, one of the editors of the *Actes*, had access to all the documents in the Archives of the Secretariat of State. As an historian he espressed his admiration of the virtues practiced by His Holiness.

After the war, Pius XII tried to repair the world-wide ravages by starting a "Save the Children Campaign." His crusade of charity was not confined to Rome. Convoys of yellow and white trucks filled with food, clothing and medical supplies followed the advancing Allied armies. In his instructions to priests who led the convoys, the Pope stressed that there was to be no discrimination of race or creed. He also allocated millions of dollars to assist displaced persons.

An article written more than fifty years ago by British convert Graham Greene sheds light on the saintly and apostolic life of Pope Pius XII. It appeared in *The Month* magazine (December 1951) entitled "The Paradox of Pope Pius."

"Like his predecessors," Greene writes, "Pius XII was the Servant of the servants of God and his aim was to serve the world, to temper the winds of hate, corruption, injustice, to give us such peace as it is possible to get here."

In his farewell to the German people in 1929, Eugenio Pacelli stated: "I go the way in which God, by the mouth of the Pontiff, commands me to go. I go this way fully conscious of my weakness, believing in Him who uses the weak to put the strong to shame. What I was, is nothing; what I am is little; but what I shall become is eternal." As Pope Pius XI placed the Red Hat on Pacelli's head, he spoke the traditional words: "Accept the Red Hat, a special sign of the Cardinal's dignity. This means that you should be ready to shed your blood and to die, if need be, in the fearless defence of our Holy Faith, for the preservation of quiet and peace among the Christian people...." A month later this Pope appointed Cardinal Pacelli as Vatican Secretary of State.

Pius XII was able to introduce an extraordinary intimacy, gentleness, a sense of love into his work and writings. Among the very few literary references, one finds Dante, Saint Augustine and Jacques-Benigne Bossuet. The Pontiff has been described as a Franciscan with a love for nature and animals. He combined his official work with pastoral work. This was seen especially during his public audiences. Unlike his encyclicals, there is an intuitive genius in his private addresses as he spoke to different groups, explaining to newly married couples that heroic energy is required in everyday life, and blessing soldiers of all sides who were welcome as pilgrims.

Greene tells the story of an army man who went to see the Pope. He had lost his only son in the war. He had no religious faith. The thought that he would never see his son again was driving him crazy. "As the Pope moved among the people, the father shouted after him. The Pope stopped and asked what he wanted. The man said he wanted to know if there was any hope of his seeing his son again. The Pope replied that that was one of those short questions which required a long answer and told his attendants to bring the man after the audience to his private room. There he sat down and for an hour explained the reasons for believing in the immortality of the soul. The man left the Pope convinced that he would see his son again and happy in the knowledge."

Recalling the Pope's Jubilee Mass in Rome, Greene concludes his article describing "the Pope in the nave of Saint Peter's ... the hand raised in a resolute blessing, the smile of deep affection, and later the Pope alone at the altar, when the cardinals who served him had stepped aside, moving with grace and precision through the motions of the Mass, doing what every priest does every day, the Servant of the servants of God, and not impossibly, one feels, a saint."

*"Our thoughts, day and night, are bent on our own great problem: how we may be able to meet this bitter trial, helping all without distinction of nationality or race, and how we may help toward restoring peace at last to tortured mankind"* *(June 2, 1944).*

# Part V: Last Will and Testament

The year 1954 was designated a "Marian Year," dedicated to Our Lady in honor of the centenary of the definition of the Dogma of the Immaculate Conception. Pius XII asked the faithful to pray for peace. His strength was failing after fifteen years of struggle and anxiety.

On February 14, while delivering a radio talk from his bed, he could not continue. However, he did not diminish his activities, nor his writings. Of the ten major addresses he prepared during this period of illness, the first dealt with television. He foresaw the dangers of this great gift of science: "Television is directed to family groups so that at any hour in any place it is capable of moving the emotions, particularly those of youth. ...The family as the cell of society must be preserved, and public authorities have the duty of taking every precaution that the home be in no way offended or disturbed. Did not even pagan Juvenal say that 'for the child one must have the utmost reverence'?"

Contrary to the advice of his doctors, the Pope insisted on officiating at the canonization of Pius X on May 29. It was too much for his frail body. He hoped to regain his strength in Castelgandolfo, where he wrote twelve more addresses. When he returned to the Vatican in November, he could neither eat nor retain food. After consultation, a team of eighteen doctors decided there was nothing they could do.

All hope was gone. On December 1, 1954, the faithful throughout Christendom were asked to pray for their spiritual leader. People of all nations and religions gathered in Saint Peter's Square also knelt in prayer, while camera crews prepared to report the Pope's death.

Pius XII knew he was dying. When he heard a Voice say, "There will be a vision!" he fell into a deep sleep. In the morning, while reciting his favorite prayer, the *Anima Christi,* he saw the Saviour standing by his bedside, "silent in all His eloquent majesty." After the last line, "In the hour of my death, call me," the Pope joyfully said, "O good Jesus! call me, order me to come to You!" The Vision disappeared.

The Pope confided this story to a few intimate friends. He did not dream it would be repeated. On November 18, 1955, it appeared in the Italian picture magazine, *Oggi.* It was written by Luigi Cavicchioli. The Vatican's answer to the media was: "No comment." The indiscreet reporter was discredited. When Pius XII learned what happened to the newspaperman for telling the truth, he ordered the Vatican press director to confirm his story.

Two days after the Vision, the Pope greeted his doctors with the words, "Good morning, gentlemen, I am happy to see you." Soon after, he wrote his Christmas message and was strong enough to deliver it over the radio. In 1955 he gave sixty major addresses and the following year there were over eighty in Latin, French, English, Italian, German, Spanish and Portuguese. The Pope had resumed his full-time schedule.

On May 15, 1956, in preparation for his death, Pope Pius XII wrote his *Last Will and Spiritual Testament.*

> *"Miserere mei Deus, secundum magnam misericordiam tuam."*
> *These words which I, knowing myself to be unworthy of them*
> *or equal to them, pronounced when I accepted with trepidation*

*my election to the supreme pontificate, I now repeat with much greater foundation at this time when the realization of the deficiencies, shortcomings and faults of so long a pontificate in an epoch so grave, brings my insufficiencies and unworthiness more clearly to my mind.*

*I humbly ask forgiveness of those whom I may have offended, harmed, or scandalized by my words and my actions.*

*I beg those to whom it pertains not to occupy themselves with or preoccupy themselves about erecting a monument to my memory. It will suffice that my poor mortal remains be simply deposited in a sacred place, the more obscure the more welcome. I need not recommend myself to prayers for my soul. I know how numerous are these which the norms of the Apostolic See provide and the piety of the faithful offer for a deceased Pope. Neither do I find need to leave a spiritual testament, as so many praiseworthy prelates normally do. The many acts and discourses decreed and pronounced by me because of my office, suffice to make my thoughts on various religious and moral questions known to anyone who might perhaps wish to know them.*

*Having set down this, I name as my universal heir the Holy Apostolic See from which I have received so much, as from a most loving Mother."*

*Pius pp. XII*

Two years later, October 9, 1958, following a brief illness while at his summer residence in Castelgandolfo, God called his faithful servant, Pope Pius XII, to his eternal reward.

The overwhelming enthusiasm and the expressions of love and respect of thousands of his contemporaries from every part of the world reflect the almost universal esteem of Pius XII's flock who believed that the Pope was a saintly representative of Christ on earth.

Sir Francis Osborne, a non-Catholic, was British minister to the Vatican from 1936 to 1947. In a letter to *The Times* of London, May 20, 1963, Ambassador Osborne wrote:

"First of all, I must emphatically declare that, so far from being a cool (which, I suppose, implies cold-blooded and inhumane) diplomatist, Pius XII was the most warmly humane, kindly, generous, sympathetic (and, incidentally, saintly) character that it has been my privilege to meet in the course of a long life. I know that his sensitive nature was acutely and incessantly alive to the tragic volume of human suffering caused by the War and, without the slightest doubt, he would have been ready and glad to give his life to redeem humanity from its consequences. And this quite irrespective of nationality or Faith...."

Rabbi Israel Zolli wrote: "No hero in all of history was more militant, more fought against, none more heroic than Pius XII in pursuing the work of true charity!...and this on behalf of all the suffering children of God."

Who can evaluate Pius XII's Crusade of Charity? At his direction, thousands of religious and lay volunteers labored day and night to save the victims of Nazism, Fascism and Communism without any thought of remuneration. Who can estimate the cost to the numberless Catholic hospitals, convents and other institutions that offered them asylum?

*"Those who guide the fate of nations should not forget that, in the words of the Scriptures, he who bears the sword is not therefore the master over the life and death of men, unless it be according to the divine law, from whence all power derives." (June 2, 1943)*

# Part VI: The "Voice" of the Public

The EWTN Interview with Raymond Arroyo on October 25, 2002, re: *Shepherd of Souls: A Pictorial Life of Pope Pius XII*, was well received. Listeners e-mailed their comments:

"Watched you on EWTN. People do hear you, Sister Margherita, and keep up your wonderful work. Those who do not hear you have succumbed to the 'errors from Russia' of which Our Lady spoke at Fatima. I had a love for Pius XII as a young girl. I believed him to be a saint."

Marie D. Marra,
Norwalk, Connecticut

"We were all there, in Germany, during World War II. I am so pleased, and so are my friends, that finally the truth is printed; the truth we always knew. It was in 1958, in Toronto, that I happened to have a conversation with a Jew. As I told him I was Catholic, he immediately said, 'Oh, you have such a wonderful Pope [Pius XII]. He has done so much for us Jews!' Where are these voices today?"

Liseselotte Eschenauer,
Toronto, Ontario, Canada

"I was in Rome during World War II and I am personally aware of the extraordinary efforts of the Church under Pope Pius XII to assist Jews and save Jewish children from their enemies. All of the recent efforts to defame His Holiness and to change history are political and can be fought best by elevating him to sainthood as early as is possible.."

Francis Paul DiBlasi, Jr.,
Naples, Florida

"I am twenty years old. . I wasn't sure how to defend Pope Pius XII. Not only that, but I wasn't sure he was blameless. But then I saw Sr. Marchione on EWTN Live, and I was struck by how well she presented him. I am convinced he did all he could, to a heroic degree, in defending both the Jews and the Faith during World War II. He was indeed a saintly man, and I would be so happy to see him canonized."

Jennifer Benjamin,
West Warwick, Rhode Island

"While growing up in Germany before and during World War II, Pope Pius XII was a source of constant strength to Catholics living during those times. Because of his example and support bishops and priests spoke out and resisted the regime. My parish in Berlin lost at least one or two young priests to concentration camps. The present campaign against this holy pope is really just an attack on the Catholic Church brought by people who were not even alive and did not live in Germany during these terrible times and who have no clue as to the conditions under which everyone lived and suffered."

Sigrid Ruedel Crane,
Vienna, Virginia

"Pope Pius XII has been a guiding force in my spiritual life and was a truly heroic spiritual figure in a world that was deeply troubled, much like our own today. I believe we need to honor this saintly figure to inspire the people today, and show that peace can be attained through prayer and thoughtful approach to all humanity."

Thomas H. Godbold II,
Portland, Oregon

"I have been a reader and defender of Pius XII since before I was a seminarian. As a priest and now a pastor, I have had many opportunities to defend the Holy Father's record and have several books in my own personal library which attest to Pope Pius' saintly life and work as pope."

Rev. Patrick Wattigny,
Metairie, Louisiana

"I will ask the intercession of our Holy Saints and Angels, as well as our Blessed Mother, to further the beatification of our humble Holy Father, Pope Pius XII."

Catherine Gallagher,
Davenport, Florida

"I was always impressed by Pope Pius XII's obvious humility and holiness. I am a freelance writer and composer. If an opportunity arises where I might write about the Pope's true courage during World War II, I will do what I can. Or perhaps I can write a song about him."

Barbara Babin Lacour,
Harahan, Louisiana

"I'm fascinated with the life of a saintly man! In my heart I know already that Pope Pius XII is a Saint."

Dominic A. M. Stefanoni,
Whiteford, Maryland

"I strongly support the beatification of Pius XII who has been unfairly represented and accused. My forthcoming book on the Italian resistance has as one aspect the role of the Italian clergy in the resistance and the role of Pius XII."

Patrick J. Gallo,
Glen Rock, New Jersey

"Pope Pius XII was an extraordinary figure of overwhelming competence who guided the Church through incredible pressures. I think he was also a holy man whom God has already honored and whom the Church should honor."

Rev. Michael P. Forbes,
Rochester, Minneapolis

"We have collected the book, and what a delight! This work to further the Beatification and Canonisation of Ven. Pius XII is so necessary. I just pray that our present Holy Father will move heaven and earth to hasten the day during his own pontificate."

Peter Bevis,
Wales, England

"Evidence proves without doubt that Pope Pius XII labored without pause for peace... We urge that you honor this holy and brave Pontiff at the soonest possible date."

Debra L. Vinnedge, Children of God for Life,
Clearwater, Florida

"When my mother gave birth to my older sister, she hemmoraged so badly that she blacked out and the last thing she remembers is seeing Pope Pius XII."

Melanie Abeyta,
Albuquerque, New Mexico

"I believe Pope Pius XII was a truly holy man and one who did so much to assist all who needed his help during the war. I look forward to his beatification."

Nanette,
Ireland

"I pray that he will become a saint, and that further review of history by this generation will prove that he was a great man for our times."

John Olgin,
El Paso, Texas

"History and time will prove Pope Pius XII's true greatness.... God truly blessed the world when He gave us Pius XII to shepherd the Church through those terrible times of World War II and the years following it."

Robert M. Donovan,
Venice, Florida

"All my life I have believed Pope Pius XII to have been a saint. When I was a child we were told he was a saint. There is no doubt in my mind about this."

Father Edward Joseph Tyler,
New South Wales, Australia

"It is an awesome privilege for me to petition the Beatification of His Holiness Pope Pius XII."

Frances M. Wires,
Cincinnati, Ohio

"I was born in January 1941, in a Catholic family. Pope Pius XII was *The Pope*, as I was growing up. I pray for his beatification."

Marie Anne Kump,
British Columbia, Canada

"I have a slide picture of His Holiness giving the blessing to the faithful in Saint Peter's Square in 1958. I was 5 years old at that time. Soon I will be 50. I have come back home to Holy Mother the Church and ask that for all that is truthful, please make Pius XII a Saint."

Robert James Groff,
Kissimmee, Florida

"I have always had a profound interest in Pope Pius XII as a person and as pope. I am happy to have now the opportunity to participate in a small way to further the process in declaring Papa Pacelli a saint in the near future."

Klaus-Werner Joseph Sirianni,
Bethesda, Maryland

"I feel that Pope Pius XII was a true gift from God, and he was challenged beyond belief with the evil that was prevalent in his time. He met that challenge and as a result the world today is better for it. God bless this effort."

Deacon Ronald R. Daigle,
South Windsor, Connecticut

"I believe that Pope Pius XII was a holy man. His death truly affected me. I did not think anyone could take his place... ."

Albert D. Cimini,<br>Mt. Ephraim, New Jersey

"As the Pope of my childhood, I have always had a deep reverence for Pope Pius XII, and to this day I feel particularly close to him, and continue to rely on his inspiration. I have been praying for his beatification."

Rosemarie Cooper,<br>Saint Lucia, West Indies

"Facts of history will remain unforgettable, especially when deposited in the hands of genuine trustees. For that sake you were divinely chosen, spiritually privileged and relatively guided... . God keep you and bless you!"

Henry E. Khoury,<br>Lakewood, Ohio

"Your EWTN presentation about Pope Pius XII was most informative as well as inspiring. Please count on me and my wife in all your efforts."

Coralie and Paul Fabijanic,<br>Cuyahoga Falls, Ohio

"I saw Pius XII many times in Piazza San Pietro when I lived in Rome in the 1950s. *Che bel ricordo!*"

Mirella E. Sacilotto Sharkey,<br>Milwaukee, Wisconsin

"Thank you for all of the valuable information on Pope Pius XII. I am the principal of Saint Ambrose Catholic Elementary School. I would like approximately 500 prayer cards for the students."

Vincent Spadoni,
Cheverly, Maryland

"I served Holy Mass the first time on the day Pope Pius XII died. One of my most vivid memories is the Solemn High Requiem Mass for the repose of his soul in my parish church a few days later. Throughout my life Pope Pius XII has been a beacon of light and truth, guiding me and keeping me loyal to the Church, despite the numerous trials we have suffered over the last forty years. God bless Pope Pius XII."

Robert Anthony Miller,
Louisville, Kentucky

"Here in England we are striving for the beatification of Pope Pius XII."

Rt. Rev. Sean Manchester,
Society of the Precious Blood

"I am praying for the cause of Pope Pius XII. He lived in difficult times and admirably followed the will of God for him. His prayer life and his devotion to his vocation are respected. He was a holy person and his work, ministry and life should be honored."

Rev. Peter Paul Brennan,
West Hempstead, New York

"Pope Pius XII served as Pope when I was in Catholic school. My mentors Rt. Rev. Monsignor Alvin P. Wagner, Rev. John McGloin, SJ, and Timothy McDonnell, SJ, always spoke of the greatness of the Roman Catholic Church under Pius XII. It will be a great honor to the memory of Pius XII for the Holy Father Pope John Paul II to make Pius XII what he was in life, a Saint.

Daniel Wyatt,<br>
Fremont, California

"I am a daughter of two Polish Holocaust survivors. My father is still alive and survived Dachau. My father was captured during the Warsaw uprising at the age of eighteen. Transported to Dachau and later to Nuengamme where he was liberated, he came to the United States in 1950 and never went back to Poland. Since the time I was a little girl (I am 35 now), I was fascinated by his stories. I always felt that I was a part of them too. It is my history, my family history that will always stay with me. I teach our six boys about the War and how important it is never to forget the atrocities committed against all humanity. I teach them we must forgive, as their grandfather taught me. Not one ounce of bitterness is in my father's heart. "The Pope did the very best he could. The accusations that he didn't do enough are so taken out of perspective. He couldn't even save his own priests from death or martyrdom. Thousands of Catholic priests and religious were killed. Saint Maximillian Kolbe and Saint Edith Stein come to mind. Are we Catholics supposed to accuse Pius for not saving his own flock? It is so unrealistic and absolutely absurd. You are right in saying he had to stay neutral, he had to be careful. To me it is no different than what our religious had to face in communist countries after the war. Even now, all over the world they are being murdered for fighting for the truths of Christ and the Catholic Church."

Yvonne Bontkowski,<br>
USA

"In his first Christmas Message in 1958, Pope John XXIII unofficially *canonized* his predecessor and referred to "our Father and Pontiff, whom we see already among God's saints in heaven."

Rupert J. Ederer.
Clarence, New York

"Please send me information about Pope Pius XII so I will be able to spread his devotion."

André Camilleri
Malta

"I did a report on Pope Pius XII for school and after doing so I learned that this Holy Man is very worthy of Sainthood!"

Ryan Cole
Walnut Ridge, Arizona

"My prayers remain with all of the faithful who have taken up this most noble cause for the canonization of Venerable Pius XII. God bless you!"

John Forgas
Beaumont, Texas

"To my fellow Christians and members of the Roman Catholic Church: Pray for peace during this time of crisis, as our esteemed brother and former Pontiff Pius XII did during his times."

Joel Jimenez
Seqjuin, Texas

"I have been praying for Pius XII's glorification since

1975. I believe it would be a fountain of grace for the Church."

Chan Slayden Casey
Houston, Texas

"The Servant of God was utterly inspirational in his personal piety, his defense of the Catholic faith, his love for souls and his angelic intelligence. He was a Pontiff who spoke and wrote clearly, succinctly and authoritatively. How we need his example and intercession today."

Rev. Edmund A. Castronovo
Oneida, New York

"Pope Pius XII was obviously a very holy man who took his Petrine Ministry very seriously, and did his best to execute it. He was indeed a Saint."

Stephen R. Jones
Carmichael, California

"It is clear to me that the slandering of Pope Pius XII is a critical element in Satan's attack on the Church. For the sake of honesty, and in defense of the Body of Christ, this holy man, who is most certainly in the loving presence of God, needs to be recognized as the hero of so many."

Leah Fisher-Toerpe
West Allis, Wisconsin

"Je réitère ici mon soutien, entier et total, à cette démarche saionte. Bénédiction à ceux qui défende la Vérité!"

Louise Marcil
Sainte-Foy, Québec

"I love His Holiness Pius XII!"

Quentin Kim
New York, New York

"I have been devoted to Pius XII for over 25 years (since I converted) and I have received great consolation from his intercession."

Chan Slayden Casey
Houston, Texas

"Pax! I am very interested about the life and works of our Pius XII. I'm looking for books. Please send me *Shepherd of Souls*. I work in a library. I will pray for your good apostolate in my Eucharistic adoration every Sunday at 17:00 p.m."

Rodrigo Ruiz
São Paulo, Brazil

"I believe it was meant for me to sign this petition. This morning while riding the train to work I was reading the May/June issue of *This Rock* magazine wherein there is an article regarding Pope Pius XII. When I got to work and turned on my computer to listen to EWTN, lo and behold, they were playing a segment of *The World Over* and guess who they were discussing? Yes, none other than Pope Pius XII! Well, that's enough of a sign for me. Now I am on a mission to learn as much as possible about the TRUTH on his life! Praised be Jesus!"

Lydia E. Morales
Central Islip, New York

"I greatly admire this venerable Pope and would like his beatification to take place without delay. Also I am interested in more information about him, which is seldom available and difficult to obtain in my country."

Waldemar Kosiedowski
Gdansk, Poland

"Please send me more information, a relic and prayer cards of Pope Pius XII."

R. Sandeep Joseph
Tamilnadu, India

"As a Roman Catholic whose great grandfather was Jewish, there is a special cause to support the beatification of Pope Pius XII. I grew up with a lot of resentment and mixed feelings hearing about the so-called *Hitler's Pope*. Now that I am older and have seen the light, I have seen the vicious lies that have been spread. I would ask the future Saint Pius XII to forgive us for not defending him. Thank you. Pius XII, pray for us!"

Timothy Joseph Andries
Breaux Bridge, Louisiana

"The book, *Shepherd of Souls,* is a real treasure. As a child, the only photos I remember of Pope Pius XII were the somber ones. What a joy it is to see the warmth of his smile! I can almost hear the lilt in his voice as he spoke to those in the photos with him, especially the children. My very favorite is the *Shepherd with the Lambs.* In that one I see the loving tenderness of Jesus as he cares for all of God the Father's little ones."

Peg Covert
Elkhart, Indiana

*"We see, indeed, a form of warfare which pro-
ceeds without intermission on its terrible way,
and piles up slaughter of such a kind that the
most bloodstained pages of history pale in
comparison with it." (December 24, 1943)*

# Part VII: Pius XII "Miracles"

## Graces Received

1. On the feast of the Solemnity of the Body and Blood of Christ, June 6, 1999, Father Ugo Musini, SJ, was celebrating the Eucharistic Liturgy in Rome, Italy. When he pronounced the words, "Broke the Bread," he suddenly felt a very acute pain in his left leg. He realized something was wrong. The pain was so severe that he began to cry and instinctively screamed in a loud voice: "What is happening to my leg?" With both arms, he leaned against the altar, so as not to fall.

With great difficulty, he continued to celebrate the Liturgy, but the pain did not cease. He then dragged himself to the sacristy. There he was surrounded by his parishioners concerned about his health. Among them was a radiologist who had been sitting in the front pew. She had recognized the intensity of Father Musini's suffering, by the sudden swelling of his jugular vein the instant he felt the pain. To calm everyone he tried to minimize the intense pain. From that moment, however, his leg was permanently painful for the following months.

Father Musini consulted another radiologist for a second opinion and also a specialist who prescribed medicine and therapy. Six months later the doctor re-examined him and stated that neither the presciptions nor the other efforts to lessen the inflammation had changed. Rather, his condition worsened. In a brutal manner, the doctor said clearly: "(1) You cannot be cured; (2) You cannot be operated; (3) You must live with this suffering for the rest of your days."

On July 20, 1999, Father Musini went to a famous physiotherapist, Dr. Ugo Zappalone who had excellent results with his patients. Notwithstanding the fact that Father Musini scrupulously performed the daily exercises suggested by Dr. Zappalone, the pain continued to increase. He did not have a moment of relief from the initial pain.

On the evening of September 12, 1999, Father Musini prayed to the Venerable Pope Pius XII whom he had always admired and to whom he was deeply devoted. As he was praying, he felt the need to stretch his leg. The pain ceased immediately. For the first time in months Father Musini fell asleep. The next morning he woke up feeling absolutely cured. He had not been able to walk since June 6th. His confreres were surprised to see him walk erectly once again.

Father Musini had new X-rays taken. The specialist compared them with the originals and said that the diagnostic results had not changed. Three years later, his condition has remained unchanged. He attributes his recovery to the intercession of Pope Pius XII.

2. Dustin Niblock wrote the following letter about his friend: "In December, 2001, I was asked to pray for a man named Gary Mangan, of Seeley's Bay, Ontario, Canada. He had Leukemia and a sort of cancer related to leukemia which caused tumors in his body. I have been devoted to Pius XII for about two years and I promised him that if he interceded for Gary and obtained his cure, I would do all within my little power to help further his cause. I have

prayed daily for Gary through the intercession of Pius XII, that Our Dear Lord would have mercy on him.

"Gary's condition worsened and I continued to pray for him. In June I was told that he had had a bone marrow transplant and they were just experimenting on him to lengthen his life. He has two young sons. Two weeks ago I heard from Mary Deryaw (the lady who asked me to pray for Gary) that she had been talking to Gary's sister who told her that Gary was better. He had gone into the hospital for another chemotherapy treatment. But they cannot find his tumors and they appear to have disappeared. He has returned to a healthy flesh colour and is doing better. Before this, he had become angry at Jesus for giving him this disease and he was very bitter. But now he is cheerful and ready to meet his Master if the call comes. He has also returned to the sacraments. I very much hope that this may be a miracle to help Pius XII on his way to be glorified in the honors of the Altar. I am truly yours in the Sacred and Immaculate Hearts." [Dustin Niblock, 194 Sweets Corners Rd., Lyndhurst, Ontario, Canada K0E-1N0]

3. The following was reported by Sister Lina Panareo, M.P.F.: "I was a novice (20 years old) with the Religious Teachers Filippini. In the summer of 1943, the inhabitants of Nettuno and Anzio were ordered to leave their homes immediately because of the imminent arrival of the Americans. We joined our Sisters in Rome. On November 3, 1943, a small group was given the privilege of a special audience with His Holiness, Pope Pius XII. We were received in a room near his study where we knelt in a semi-circle around the Holy Father. He greeted us in a fatherly manner and walked toward each one of us who had sought refuge in Rome. With words of encouragement and expressive ges-

tures, we noted the profound love and compassion he felt for his flock.

"When the Pope arrived in front of me, he asked where I came from. Hearing I was from Otranto, and learning that I had no news about my relatives, he assured me that, through the Vatican, he would obtain news about my parents. He then asked if I had any brothers in the war zone. I told him that one of them had volunteered. He was 17 years old. I recall with emotion that the Holy Father placed his hand on my head saying, 'He will return; he will return!' During three long years of anxiety, my parents had lost all hope of seeing their son alive. Sustained by the words of the Pope, I remained confident. I knew we would again embrace my brother. On December 26, 1946, after the long prison term he endured in Yugoslavia, my brother returned home. Pius XII's prophetic words during that unforgettable audience in 1943, were finally fulfilled."

4. Eugenio Osti, from Italy wrote: "I am an old medical doctor and surgeon, a practicing Catholic devoted to the memory of Pope Pius XII. For years during my professional life and later, in moments of uncertainty, confusion, sufferings both physical and moral, I have always invoked the intercession of Pope Pacelli before the throne of the Lord and very often I have received insights, comfort and serenity. I am reading your new book and it consoles me greatly." (Dott. Eugenio Osti, Medico Chirurgo, Via Piaggio, 67-6, Genoa, Italy 16136.)

5. Gennaro Giammarino, III, from Roslyn Heights, New York, wrote on March 5, 2003: "His Holiness Pope Pius XII was a wonderful compassionate and caring man who helped save the Jewish People during the War. I am 35 years old and

have been ill with Cancer for 11 years. Thanks to prayers to Pope Pius alone, I am now cancer free, but disabled. I credit Pope Pius with the miracle of saving my life more than six times. I have come to peace with God, through my prayers to His Holiness and believe without a doubt, that he watches over me and protects me. I am permanently disabled, but that is a small price to pay to keep my life. If Pope Pius XII didn't intercede for me, I would have died 10 years ago. Please beatify him and make him a Saint. ...My grandfather knew him and loved him."

On the same day, Michael and Marianna Giammarino from Lynbrook, New York, wrote: "Through the intercession of Pope Pius XII, our son's life was spared from cancer in the darkest hour of our lives." Mary M. Basile and Gennaro Giammarino, Jr., from North Miami Beach, Florida, also commented: "Our nephew was cured from cancer through our prayers to His Holiness, Pope Pius XII."

*"Peace is a 'good' so precious, so desirable and so desired that every effort to defend it, even at the cost of sacrificing one's own aspirations, is a 'good' well spent" (December 24, 1957).*

# Part VIII: The "Voice" of His Successors

In a world of unprecedented evil and violence, Pope Pius XII made every effort to alleviate the human suffering of the Second World War and laid the foundations for the great insights of the Second Vatican Council. His spirituality and theological vision, his compassionate commitment to the poor, the sick and the victims of Nazism, Fascism and communism, cannot be ignored.

When Angelo Giuseppe Roncalli was Apostolic Nuncio in Istanbul, he wrote in his *Diary* (October 10, 1941) about an audience with Pope Pius XII. He also made known the fact that he followed the Pope's directives with regard to saving the Jews.

In his 1958 Christmas Message, soon after his election, Pope John XXIII referred to his predecessor as "our Father and Pontiff, whom we see already among God's saints in heaven. The triple title *Doctor Optimus, Ecclesiae sanctae lumen, divinae legis amator* would be most suitable to his memory" (Michael Chinigo, *The Teachings of John XXIII*, 1967).

As far as his relationship to the promotion of world peace, the name of Pope John XXIII cannot be separated from that of his immediate predecessor, Pope Pius XII. On May 10, 1963, international headlines spoke about the Cuban missile crisis and Pope John XXIII's mediation. He was awarded the Balzan Peace Prize, "for his activity in favor of brotherhood between all men and all people, and his appeals for peace and good will in the recent diplomatic intervention." Seated in the Vatican Throne Room as he gave his acceptance speech, the Pope said that the award was as much for his predecessors as for himself: the five Popes of his lifetime had all "worked untiringly to maintain, develop, and consolidate peace among men." (John Jay Hughes, *Pontiffs: Popes Who Shaped History*, Our Sunday Visitor, Huntington, IN, 1994, p. 286.)

During the Second Vatican Council John XXIII and Paul VI followed the leadership of Pius XII who had played not only a key role in preparing for it, but whose words were the most frequently quoted after Holy Scripture.

During World War II, Archbishop Angelo Giuseppe Roncalli was concerned about those who were suffering under the Nazis, Fascists and Communists. He sent thousands of immigration certificates, including Palestine immigration papers to Monsignor Angelo Rotta, the Papal Nuncio in Budapest. To guarantee their safety, hundreds of Jews were "baptized" in the air-raid shelters of Budapest. Many escaped to Palestine, thanks to the immigration certificates forwarded by the Archbishop. All this was done in consonance with Pius XII's directives.

On the seventieth anniversary of Leo XIII's *Rerum Novarum*, John XXIII adapted the general teaching of the Church on social problems in his encyclical, *Mater et Magistra* (1961). His teaching on private property, on socialization, on international life, and on the dignity of the individual was recognized. Emphasis was placed on the duties of the rich nations toward the poorer, and wealth being divided among the nations of the world. Two years later, the encyclical *Pacem in Terris* created a stir throughout the world. It was

110

based on international life and the dignity of the individual: equal rights for men and women; equality of different races; rights of minorities; respect for ethnic characteristics; racialism was condemned; the work of the United Nations was commended.

In his 1963 encyclical, *Pacem in Terris*, following Pius XII's policy of peace founded on justice, John XXIII stressed that there are no inferior peoples, no inferior races: "Truth calls for the elimination of every trace of racial discrimination. All men are equally noble in natural dignity." He urged the world to remember that the Church was coming to the aid of World Peace by means of the General Council directed toward true brotherhood.

When he died, U Thant, Secretary-General, United Nations General Assembly wrote: "In identifying himself so unreservedly with the cause of peace and international understanding, John XXIII became the very embodiment of mankind's own aspirations in this uncertain period of history....The thinking and actions of John XXIII were unfailingly guided by a full measure of confidence in the potentialities of mankind. Let this confidence be a source of inspiration to us all, so that we, too, may usefully serve the cause of peace and understanding among men."

No better tribute can be paid to Pius XII than the fact that, in the encyclical *Pacem in Terris,* John XXIII repeated the words of his predecessor: "*Nothing is lost by peace; everything may be lost by war.*" John XXIII also reminded the world about Pius XII's radio broadcast on Christmas Eve in 1941, that "in the field of a new order founded on moral principles, there is no room for violation of freedom, integrity and security." The flame John XXIII enkindled has indeed inspired his successors, Paul VI and John Paul II who picked up on his legacy and faced world conflicts from Vietnam to the Balkans to the Gulf to the present war with Iraq, and the never-ending strife in the Holy Land.

In 1963, Pope Paul VI decisively established the falsehood of Rolf Hochhuth's allegations against the Catholic Church when he ordered the opening of the Vatican archives and selected Jesuit Church historians Pierre Blet, Angelo Martini, Burkhart Schneider and Robert A. Graham. The monumental work of these historians resulted in the publication of eleven volumes of the *Acts and Documents of the Holy See Relative to the Second World War.*

No Pope throughout history did more—to create closer relations with the Jewish community, to oppose anti-Semitism, and to make certain that the evils of the Holocaust never again occur— than Pope John Paul II whose voice has been heard again and again as he pleads for courageous workers willing to serve and suffer, in the footsteps of Christ, for peace.

Relations between the Catholic Church and the Jewish people are marked by mutual respect and understanding. Pope John Paul II visited the Chief Rabbi of Rome in 1986 and declared that "the Jews are our dearly beloved brothers," and indeed "our elder brothers in faith." He requested forgiveness for past sins by Christians against Jews. He established full diplomatic relations between the Holy See and the State of Israel. A survivor of both Nazi and Communist oppression himself, John Paul II has consistently praised Pope Pius XII for his heroic leadership during World War II, and led the cause for his canonization.

On Palm Sunday, March 28, 1999, John Paul II declared to a crowd in Saint Peter's Square: "The Pope stands with the people who suffer, and cries out to all: it is always time for peace! It is never too late to meet and negotiate!" In his Easter message, he pleaded: "Peace is possible, peace is a duty, peace is a prime responsibility of everyone!" On May 3, he stated: "I raise my voice again, in the name of God, that this attack of man against man come to an end, that the instruments of destruction and death be stopped, that all channels of aid be activated to help those who are forced to flee their land amid unspeakable atrocities... ."

*"For those who have allowed themselves to be seduced by the advocates of violence, there is but one road to salvation: to repudiate once and for all the idolatry of absolute nationalism, the pride in origin, race and blood." (March 19, 1945)*

# Part IX: Epilogue

"Pius XII did everything; all that he had to do, all that he could do, and he did everything well." This statement was written by Vatican secretary of state, Cardinal Domenico Tardini in his book, *Pio XII* (Tipografia Poliglotta Vaticana, 1960, 180 pp.).

This book is a marvelous source of information and an extraordinary testimonial by one of Pius XII's closest collaborators. It begins with a eulogy by the then Cardinal Angelo Roncalli given in Saint Mark's Basilica, Venice, on October 11, 1958. The future Pope John XXIII recalls the magisterium of Pius XII who "adapted himself to modern thought and progress." He stated that history will recall his example, his messages. As leader of the Catholic Church, his name would be listed among the great and most popular of modern history. He concluded with a prayer: "You were, the *Pastor Angelicus* and you guided us along the path of eternal life; you were the defender of our country, in our most tragic hours; ...bless our homes, families, priests, our poor, our suffering, our children. Oh, unforgettable, saintly Father, *sit super nos semper benedictio tua. Amen.*"

The following year, October 20, 1959, Cardinal Tardini, in the presence of Pope John XXIII, spoke about the life and works of Pius XII. He mentioned that, on the seventeenth anniversary of his papacy, as he approached the Pope to express his wishes, Pius XII looked at him with tearful eyes and, shaking his hand, murmured: "My dear Monsignor, this is a crown of thorns!"

Cardinal Tardini continued: "The Lord was generous with his gifts. Pope Pius XII was intelligent, brilliant, versatile; he was always ready and generous; he had a formidable memory. To this one can add many beautiful natural qualities: ardent piety, limitless charity, absolute dedication to his duty; he worked intensely without respite; his spirit of sacrifice was heroic.

"His Holiness possessed a rich treasure of knowledge, of observations, of studies; of difficulties he overcame, of battles he fought, of agreements he laboriously negotiated and happily concluded. Briefly, his many, many experiences, were one more precious than the other, such as rarely can be found in the life of one man.

"Pius XII's great faith dominated his life. He appeared to all as a peaceful person, often smiling, always amiable, kind and friendly. Constantly united with God, he succeeded in keepng calm during difficult times, serene during stormy periods; although preoccupied, he was not disturbed; anguished, but not discouraged; nor did the most bitter battles alter or diminish the sweetness of his interior peace. He was always pleasant and enjoyed vivacious conversations; like a humanist of the Renaissance, he appreciated literary expressions; as a true Roman, he loved witty and comic remarks. When laughing, his mouth was open, his eyes vibrant, his arms extended, and he assumed the expression of a happy child. His meek temperament made him naturally dislike arguments, but when truth, justice, and the good of souls were concerned, he became a fearless fighter. He will go down in history as a Pontiff who was a wise reformer and brave innovator.

116

"Pius XII was a voice of truth, of justice, of love. He was a holy person, a symbol of mercy and of hope during a period of lies, despair and hatred. Everyone appreciated his intelligence and his extraordinary capacity to comprehend the dangers of Nazism and his efforts to alleviate the sufferings of humanity. His messages attempted to unite the world. His contemporaries listened to his inspiring words, as he spoke of brotherhood, of love, and of peace at a time of spiritual poverty and material destruction of exceptional dimensions."

The words of Cardinal Tardini in his book, *Pio XII* (pp. 96-97), are appropriate: "Who can ever forget the grandiose and characteristic gesture with which Pius XII concluded his audiences? Slender and erect, the Pope fixed his eyes toward heaven. It was a gesture of *imploring*. With arms outstretched, the Pontiff seemed to embrace all humanity in a paternal embrace. It was a gesture of *blessing*. With open arms and extended hands, that body seemed almost rigid, and gave the impression of a figure on a crucifix. It was a gesture of *immolation*. Pius XII was able to make his the words of the Apostle: 'I am nailed with Christ to the Cross.' (Galatians, 2, 19.) In his sorrows and in his sufferings, Pius XII was a generous victim who consumed himself in the holocaust of his daily sacrifice. If his crown was a crown of thorns, the Cross was his support, his refuge, his comfort. Thus, once again, in the luminous heaven of the Church, the Cross was for a saintly and great Pontiff, a throne of majesty, a seat of truth, a vessel of glory and of triumph."

The vilification of the person of Pope Pius XII and the denigration of our present Pope John Paul II affects the Magisterium of the Catholic Church. Both Popes are accused of "silence." The Vatican chastised the Anti-Defamation League for its ads in the *New York Times* and the *Inter-*

*national Herald Tribune.* On May 18, 2001, in a letter to Abraham Foxman obtained by *The Jewish Week*, Walter Cardinal Kasper, head of the Commission for Religious Relations with the Jews, defended John Paul II: "To defame the Holy Father by attributing 'silence' to him is quite unjust and cannot go uncontested. ...It wounds our relationship."

Pope John Paul II repeatedly defended Pope Pius XII. In 1987, during a meeting with Jewish leaders, he recalled "how deeply Pius XII felt about the tragedy of the Jewish people, and how hard and effectively he worked to assist them during the Second World War."

In his Christmas radio messages of '41, '42, and '43, the Pope denounced theories that attribute rights to "a particular race." He revealed that "hundreds of thousands of people, through no fault of theirs, sometimes only because of nationality or race, were destined to die."

One cannot speak of the "silence" of Pius XII. Rather one must speak of his "prudence." No one can deny his actions—sheltering Jews in the Vatican and in the papal summer home in Castelgandolfo; ordering that convents, monasteries, hospitals and schools shelter Jews; issuing of false baptismal certificates, false identity papers and passports as well as providing money for ransom and travel to other countries. These actions, in addition to appeals to Italian and German authorities on behalf of particular Jews and Jewish communities, have been acknowledged and should not be underestimated.

In the book, *Pio XII: Il Papa degli Ebrei,* historian Andrea Tornielli cites the Evangelical Bishop of Berlin, Otto Dibelius: "What this Pope did or did not do, what he suffered or did not suffer, and the conflicts he conscientiously overcame before God, can be judged only by one who has had such a responsibility, and has learned what it means to profess the Christian faith and the Ten Commandments while in the frightening atmosphere of a totalitarian state and controlled by such a government." (Piemme, 2001, p. 199)

The charge of Pius XII's "silence" with regard to the Nazis is simply not true. Certain Polish bishops, exiled in London, called for stronger statements by the Pontiff, while those who remained in Poland and had to deal with the Nazis, cautioned the Pope to refrain from "speaking out" against Hitler, lest his words be used as a pretext for savage reprisals. In a letter to Pope Pius XII, dated October 28, 1942, Archbishop Adam Stefan Sapieha stated: "It displeases us greatly that we cannot communicate Your Holiness' letters to our faithful, but it would furnish a pretext for further persecution and we have already had victims suspected of communicating with the Holy See."

Writing to Bishop Konrad von Preysing of Berlin, Pius XII explained: "We leave it to the local bishops to weigh the circumstances in deciding whether or not to exercise restraint, *ad maiora mala vitanda* [to avoid greater evil]. This would be advisable if the danger of retaliatory and coercive measures would be imminent in cases of public statements by the bishop. Here lies one of the reasons We Ourselves restrict Our public statements. The experience We had in 1942 with documents which We released for distribution to the faithful gives justification, as far as We can see, for Our attitude."

Despite Pius XII's peace efforts, the Allies would accept nothing short of Germany's unconditional surrender, even though it meant prolonging the Holocaust. Historian John Toland reported: "The Church, under the Pope's guidance, had already saved the lives of more Jews than all other churches, religious institutions and rescue organizations combined, and was presently hiding thousands of Jews in monasteries, convents and Vatican City itself.

"The record of the Allies was far more shameful. The British and Americans, despite lofty pronouncements, had not only avoided taking any meaningful action but gave sanctuary to few persecuted Jews. The Moscow Declaration of that year—signed by Roosevelt, Churchill and Stalin—methodically listed Hitler's victims as Polish, Italian, French, Dutch, Belgian, Norwegian, Soviet and Cretan. The curious omission of Jews (a policy emulated by the U.S. Office of War Information) was protested vehemently but uselessly by the World Jewish Congress. By the simple expedient of converting the Jews of Poland into Poles, and so on, the Final Solution was lost in the Big Three's general classification of Nazi terrorism" (Doubleday, NY, 1976, pp. 760-61).

However, in Monsignor Montini's "Notes" (*Actes*, Vol. 3, Letter 102), dated January 19, 1940, the Pope's intervention is clearly stated: "Pius XII ordered that information on the condition of the Church in Poland be circulated via German transmissions of Vatican Radio."

In his book, *I dilemmi e i silenzi di Pio XII*, historian Giovanni Miccoli reconstructs the facts and presents the mental attitudes, maneuvers and difficulties of the Vatican Curia during World War II. Miccoli states that the Vatican avoided taking a position that would violate its neutrality. "By condemning Nazism, Pius XII would have endangered millions of Catholics and thousands of German priests. He would have jeopardized, as well, the safety of the Jews in Rome, which was the center of Fascist Italy occupied by the Germans. To take a position could have signified that the war would be transformed into a crusade.... It meant going to battle with serious and dangerous consequences. Ultimately the results would block the action of persuasion, assistance and peacemaking that was the role of the pontiff" (Rizzoli, 2000, p. 407).

120

Pius XII was far from silent. In *Summi Pontificatus* (1939) and *Mystici Corporis* (1943), as well as in his Christmas messages and his June 2, 1943 address to the Cardinals, he clearly repudiated Nazi racist ideology. He ordered papal representatives to intervene in Belgium, Bulgaria, France, Greece, Holland, Hungary, Rumania, Slovakia, Spain and Turkey to stem the deportation of innocent victims to death camps. He took great risks to protect and save as many Jews as he could by sheltering them in Vatican buildings and releasing monasteries and convents from the rule of cloister.

There is no proof that a formal denunciation of Hitler and the Nazis would have been of any help to the Jews. The Church would have been treated as an enemy power and the Nazis would have invaded the Vatican and searched Catholic buildings everywhere for Jewish refugees. Pope Pius XII's own assessment was: "No doubt a protest would have gained the praise and respect of the civilized world, but it would have submitted the poor Jews to an even worse persecution." (Quoted by Rabbi Joseph I. Lichten in his Introduction to Graham, *Pius XII's Defense of Jews and Others*, pp. 2-3; See also Pinchas Lapide, *Three Popes and the Jews*, p. 247.)

Owen Chadwick, a well-respected British historian, wrote in *The Tablet* of London (March 28, 1998) that the propaganda against Pius XII was promoted by the Communists, "propaganda in the first instance by Stalin's men in the Cold War. …Stalin had a political need to make this Pope contemptible."

The fact remains that Pius XII's voice was heard. He was the object of unanimous admiration and sincere gratitude. Who can deny that Vatican Radio explicitly condemned "the immoral principles of Nazism" (October 15, 1940), and the "the wickedness of Hitler" citing Hitler by name (March 10, 1941). The London *Times* praised Pius XII: "There is no room for doubt. He condemns the worship of force … and the persecution of the Jewish race" (October 1, 1942).

Soon after, *The Tablet* of London reported that Nazi leader Goebbels issued pamphlets in many languages condemning Pius XII as a "pro-Jewish Pope" (October 24, 1942). Jewish scholar Jenö Levai, who served as an expert witness at Adolf Eichmann's War Crimes Trial, insisted that bishops of the Catholic Church intervened again and again on the instructions of the Pope, "…the one person who did more than anyone else to halt the dreadful crime and alleviate its consequences, is today made the scapegoat for the failures of others" (*Hungarian Jewry and the Papacy: Pius XII Was Not Silent*, Sands and Company, London, 1968).

Monsignor John Patrick Carroll-Abbing, founder of Boys' Town and Girls' Town of Italy, was among the Vatican officials who, at the explicit instructions of the Pope, helped shelter and feed thousands of Jews during the German occupation of Rome. He recorded the Vatican's vast rescue network in his autobiography, *But for the Grace of God* (Delacorte Press, 1965).

In a taped interview with William Doino, Jr., Monsignor Carroll-Abbing confirmed these facts and described how the Pontiff personally ordered him and other Vatican officials to rescue Jews, and make sure to do "whatever was necessary" to allow them to practice their Jewish faith in private, according to their sacred rites. Responding to questions about the lack of papal protests, he added: "Pius XII was not silent at all! This is one of the great falsehoods of the twentieth century. He was outspoken in his condemnation of Fascist and Nazi atrocities…. I worked with Fathers Pfeiffer and Benoît, my assistant, Monsignor Vitucci, and Cardinals Dezza, Palazzini, Maglione, Montini, and Tardini. …I repeat, we acted on direct orders and instructions of the Holy Father."

In *Pius XII and the Second World War* (Paulist Press, 1997), Pierre Blet, SJ, concluded: "Several years later Pius XII returned to these years of fire and sword in a speech to nurses given in May 1952. He asked the question: 'What should we have done that we have not done?' The Pope was saying that he was conscious of what he had accomplished to prevent the war, to alleviate its sufferings, to reduce the number of its victims—everything he thought he could do. The documents [the *Actes*], in so far as they allow one to probe the human heart, come to the same conclusion. As for results, to affirm that the Pope himself or some other person in his place might have been able to do more is to depart from the field of history in order to venture into the undergrowth of suppositions and dreams."

Pius XII was not a "silent" Pope. The wisdom of his words and actions is supported by the evidence. In an interview, Los Angeles radio host Bill Handel allowed his father, a Jew, to report that he was saved by the Pope during World War II. The actions of Pope Pius XII and the Catholic Church in trying to save Jews hunted down by the Nazis have been both praised and criticized. Pius XII was a symbol of hope and love during a period of despair and hatred.

Among recent books condemning Pius XII and portraying the Catholic Church as an oppressive, anti-Semitic force are: John Cornwell's *Hitler's Pope: The Secret History of Pius XII* (1999); Michael Phayer's *The Catholic Church and the Holocaust, 1930-1945* (1999); Gary Wills' *Papal Sin: Structures of Deceit* (1999); James Carroll's *Constantine's Sword: The Church and the Jews: A History* (2000); Susan Zuccotti's *Under His Very Windows: The Vatican and the Holocaust in Italy* (2001); Daniel Jonah Goldhagen's *A Moral Reckoning: the Catholic Church during the Holocaust and Today* (2002).

Michael Novak has rightly stated: "Our faith is not in men, but in God. So there is no need for Catholics to be defensive about Pius XII. But there is need to defend the truth… . The more some of us who were earlier predisposed to blame Pius XII study this question, the better Pius XII looks and the weaker the case against him."

Speaking in Saint Louis, Missouri, January 27, 1999, Pope John Paul II stated: "If you want Peace, work for Justice. If you want Justice, defend Life. If you want Life, embrace the Truth—the Truth revealed by God." As early as 1940, the Vatican published reports on the Church in Germany and the slaughter of Poles. Catholic defenders maintain that the Pope knew what the Nazis were doing not only to Jews, but also to Catholic priests and nuns, Gypsies, Slavs and other groups being persecuted. His strategy of helping behind the scenes was considered by his contemporaries to have been wise. He enunciated moral principles, avoided provocations, strove for impartiality among belligerents and issued information about Nazi atrocities through the Vatican Radio and *L'Osservatore Romano*. In addition, he implemented the most extensive relief effort during and after the war and saved thousands of Jews and other refugees.

Pope Pius XII had to deal with Adolf Hitler and the Holocaust, Benito Mussolini and Fascism, the occupation of Rome by the Nazis, the development of atomic warfare, and the spread of Communism across eastern Europe. The front-page caption of the *New York Times* (September 16, 1939) was in very large print: "Pope Condemns Dictators, Treaty Violators, Racism; Urges Restoring of Poland." His entire encyclical, *Summi Pontificatus* was printed on pages 8 and 9. It was a powerful attack on totalitarianism and racism. Pius XII not only publicly defended his Jewish brethren explicitly using the word "Jew," but did so in the context of condemning racism by quoting Saint Paul (Col. 3:10-11).

There is a vast wealth of new evidence for the work of Pope Pius XII in fighting against the violent anti-Semitic policies of the Nazis and seeking the rescue of the Jewish people from under their control. Unbiased historians do not accept the baseless charges claiming the Pope was silent on the unfolding tragedy or was morally culpable, or even was himself anti-Semitic.

A letter written in 1923 by the future Pope Pius XII shows his early opposition to Nazi anti-Semitism. Dated November 14, 1923, the letter was written by then Archbishop Pacelli, the Holy See's ambassador in Bavaria, in southern Germany, to Cardinal Pietro Gasparri, Vatican secretary of state under Pope Pius XI. The letter refers to Adolf Hitler's failed attempt to take over the local government in Munich in the National Socialist Party's putsch of November 9, 1923. Contrary to the allegations of a number of recent authors on the relations between Pius XII and the Nazis, the letter denounces the National Socialist movement as an anti-Catholic threat and notes that the cardinal of Munich had already condemned acts of persecution against Bavaria's Jews.

A letter, warning the National Socialist government not to persecute the Jews (dated April 4, 1933), was signed by Cardinal Pacelli and sent at the instruction of Pius XI to Monsignor Cesare Orsenigo, the apostolic nuncio in Germany.

This letter reflects the good relations that the Vatican had with Jewish officials and its desire to respond to their request. It also shows that he did speak in favor of the Jews: "Important Israeli personalities have appealed to the Holy Father to ask for his intervention against the danger of anti-

125

Semitic excesses in Germany.... Since the Holy See must carry out its mission of universal peace and charity toward all men, regardless of their social or religious condition, by offering its charitable assistance if necessary, the Holy Father asks Your Excellency to see if and how it is possible to help them."

The opening of the Vatican Archives has already proven that accusations against Pius XI and Pius XII are baseless. Documents reveal that in 1933, as Secretary of State, Pacelli reviewed Nunzio Cesare Orsenigo's New Year's discourse and by secret code told him to remove the words "Leader of the German people" and to eliminate a paragraph that praised Hitler. In 1936, when invited by Hitler to attend the Nazi Congress, the Nunzio again sought advice. So that he would not be obliged to attend, Pacelli suggested that he take a vacation so that he could absent himself. Pacelli corrected the Nunzio's communications and told him not to participate with the Diplomatic Corps. Other corrections prove that Pacelli was not sympathtic toward Hitler whom he considered possessed by the devil and even attempted to exorcize him.

Historians and archivists confirm the authenticity of this document which demonstrates that, early on, the Vatican protested on behalf of Jews in Nazi Germany. It confirms the testimony of Father Robert Leiber who, in 1962, wrote an article on Pius XI's papal encyclical of 1937, *Mit Brennender Sorge,* which appeared in the German periodical *Stimmen der Zeit.* Leiber wrote: "It is significant that the first initiative of the Holy See toward the government in Berlin concerned the Jews. As early as April 4, 1933, ten days after the Enabling Act, the Apostolic Nuncio in Berlin was ordered to intervene with the government of the Reich on behalf of the Jews and point out all the dangers involved in an anti-Semitic policy." The Catholic Church, therefore, did not simply protest on behalf of Church interests during negotiations of the Concordat, but protested on behalf of persecuted Jews when the new Hitler regime announced a major boycott of Jewish businesses.

Jewish descendants, even if baptized, were deprived of their German citizenship. In 1934, when the Nazis initiated their first large-scale massacre, Cardinal Pacelli had the Vatican newspaper, *L'Osservatore Romano,* unequivocally condemn the Nazi crimes in three articles, proclaiming that "National socialism better deserved the name of *national terrorism,* and that like all movements which resort to terrorism, it sprang from a gang rather than from a party."

In a letter dated March 12, 1935 to Cardinal Carl Joseph Schulte of Cologne, Pacelli attacked the Nazis as "false prophets with the pride of Lucifer," labeling them "bearers of a new faith and a new gospel' who were attempting to create a "mendacious antimony" between faithfulness to the Church and the Fatherland."

As Pope, Eugenio Pacelli was not silent and numerous protests and interventions were made through Vatican nuncios and ambassadors. In his book, *The Vatican and Its Role in World Affairs* (p. 147), Charles Pichon explained that Pius XII's speeches on behalf of victims of Nazi terrorism were clear: "The pontifical texts condemned most strongly the antisemitic persecutions, the oppression of invaded lands, the inhuman conduct of the war, and also the deification of earthly things which were made into idols: the Land and the Race, the State and the Class."

Truth and justice demand a re-evaluation of the attacks against Pius XII, claiming "silence," "moral culpability," or "anti-Semitism." In response to the malicious accusations against Pius XII, several Paulist Press books provide the testimony of Jews and Catholics, and also reproduce valuable Vatican documents that help our understanding of the Holocaust: *Yours Is a Precious Witness: Memoirs of Jews and Catholics in Wartime Italy* (1997); *Pope Pius XII: Architect for Peace* (2000), *Consensus and Controversy: Defending Pope Pius XII* (2002). In response to the malicious accusations that have been leveled against Pius XII, *Shepherd of Souls: A Pictorial Life of Pope Pius XII* (2002) not only provides the testimony of Jews and Catholics, but also reproduces valuable Vatican documents that help our understanding of the Holocaust and promote the truth about a saintly twentieth-century Pope.

An article in the "Corriere della Sera," dated September 20, 1967, reports what one Jew said before fleeing to Spain and what all Jews really expected from His Holiness: "None of us wanted the Pope to speak out openly. We were all fugitives hidden in convents and monasteries and the Gestapo would have only intensified their search for us. This is what we thought and we still believe that today. Pius XII had to choose between denouncing the Nazis or saving the lives of thousands of Jews and Christians. He chose to save precious lives."

On October 29, 1944, Jan Hermann and Dr. Max Pereles, the camp elders of the Ferramonti-Tarsia concentration camp, went to the Vatican to thank Pope Pius XII and gave him a letter which read in part: "While our brothers were hunted, imprisoned and threatened with death in almost every country in Europe, because they belonged to the Jewish people, Your Holiness has not only sent us large and generous gifts … but also fearlessly raised his universally respected voice, in the face of our powerful enemies, in order to defend openly our rights to the dignity of man. …When we were threatened with deportation to Poland, in 1942,

Your Holiness extended a fatherly hand to protect us, and stopped the transfer of the Jews interned in Italy, thereby saving us from almost certain death."

No longer can the Catholic world tolerate the careless innuendoes and unfounded accusations that have been leveled against Pope Pius XII's reputation as a courageous and holy Shepherd of Souls. He was a saintly man, a scholar, a man of peace, a committed defender and protector of the victims of war and hatred which drenched Europe in blood during World War II.

# Part X: Chronology of Pope Pius XII's Life 1876-1958

1876    Born in Rome of Virginia Graziosi, wife of Filippo Pacelli, March 2.
        Baptized Eugenio Maria Giuseppe Giovanni, March 4.
1880    Eugenio Pacelli entered Kindergarten, and then attended Elementary School.
1886    Received First Holy Communion.
1891    Studied at the Ennio Quirino Visconti Lyceum.
1894    Entered the Capranica Seminary in October; enrolled also at Gregorian University.
1895    Suffered a physical setback, requiring him to live at home, while continuing his studies.
        Registered in the Sapienza School of Philosophy and Letters and at the Papal Athenaeum of St. Apollinaris for Theology. He received the Baccalaureate and Licentiate degrees *summa cum laude.*
1899    Ordained a priest, April 2.
        Assigned as curate to the Chiesa Nuova.
        Continued studies for a doctorate in Canon Law and Civil Law at the Apollinaris.
1901    Served as a research aide in the Office of the Congregation of Extraordinary Ecclesiastical Affairs.
1904    Became a Papal Chamberlain with the title of Monsignor.
1905    Became a Domestic Prelate.
1910    Represented the Holy See at the Coronation of King George V in London.
1911    Appointed Assistant Secretary of the Congregation of Extraordinary Ecclesiastical Affairs, March 7.

1912    Became pro-Secretary of the Congregation of Extraordinary Ecclesiastical Affairs, June 20.
1914    Became Secretary of the said Congregation, February 1.
1917    Appointed Nuncio to Bavaria, Germany, April 20.
        Consecrated Bishop and elevated to the rank of Archbishop, May 13.
        Presented his credentials to Ludwig III, King of Bavaria, May 28.
1920    Appointed first Apostolic Nunzio of Germany, June 22.
1924    Signed a Concordat with Bavaria, March 29, ratified by the Bavarian Parliament on January 15, 1925.
1925    Left Munich for residence in Berlin.
1929    Concluded a Concordat with Prussia, June 14, ratified August 14.
        Recalled to Rome and received a Cardinal's hat on December 16.
1930    Appointed Secretary of State, February 7.
        Became archpriest of the Vatican Basilica, March 25.
1934    Presided as Papal Legate at the International Eucharistic Congress in Buenos Aires, Argentina, October 10-14.
1935    Spoke at Lourdes, April 25-28, as Pope Pius XI's delegate to France for the closing days of the jubilee year honoring the nineteenth centenary of Redemption.
1936    Arrived in the United States of America on the *Conte di Savoia,* October 8, for an "unofficial" trip covering some eight thousand miles chiefly by plane, as he made an in-depth study of the American Church.
        Invited to a luncheon at Hyde Park after President Franklin D. Roosevelt's re-election.
1937    Traveled to France in July as Cardinal-Legate to consecrate and dedicate the new basilica in Lisieux during the Eucharistic Congress.
1938    Presided at the International Eucharistic Congress in Budapest, May 25-30.
1939    Elected Pope, on March 2, taking the name of Pius XII.
        Received the papal tiara, March 12. Issued his first encyclical, *Summi Pontificatus* (On the Unity of Human Society—an

attack on totalitarianism—October 20, after the Nazis' invasion of Poland, September 1).

1943    Issued *Mystici Corporis Christi*, June 29.

Comforted the injured, administered the Last Rites, distributed money to those in need of food and clothing when American bombers dropped hundreds of tons of explosives on Rome, July 19.

Issued *Divino Afflante Spiritu* (Biblical Studies), September 30.

1947    Issued *Fulgens Radiatur* (14th centenary of St. Benedict), March 21.

Issued *Mediator Dei* (Liturgy of the Church), November 20.

1950    Defined dogma of the Assumption of the Virgin Mary, November 1, with a Papal Bull (*Munificentissimus Deus*).

Issued *Humani Generis*, August 12.

1953    Signed a Concordat with Spain, August 27.

1956    Reformed the Holy Week Liturgy.

1957    Issued *Fidei Donum* (Future of Africa), April 21.

1958    Death of Pope Pius XII, October 9.

# Part XI: A. Words of Wisdom

The Catholic Church is the faithful depository of the teaching of Divine Wisdom. An abridged guide to the writings and spirit of Christian culture, as expressed by Pope Pius XII, may be found in *The Mind of Pius XII,* an anthology by Robert C. Pollack, (New York: Crown Publishers, Inc. 1955). It offers thoughts, writings and messages on religious and secular topics taken from the papal documents of Pius XII.

The author states in his *Foreword* that humanism implied by Christianity has a depth as fathomless as the human soul itself, made to the image and likeness of God. We can do no better than quote the Pope himself: "Look at the Cross; look at all those who have suffered! By word and example Jesus taught men; by miracles He went about doing good; but, by His Passion and Cross, He saved the world."

Directives for the totality of human life are covered against the background of modern knowledge in the Pope's communications and discourses. Religion offers "a vision of the whole, of the present as of the future, of matter as of spirit, of time as of eternity." It gives a powerful presentation of human dignity and of man's aspiration to truth and goodness.

The Church should look back with pride on her past and on the treasure of her teachings. Pius XII's writings continue to guide the Church. Concerned with its development, he dealt with all topics: education, economics, the social question. He was aware of "the agonizing dilemma between youth and old age" and of the "contradictory aspects of historical evolution." His profound sense of history gives new courage and confidence to all who believe in unchanging truth.

The Church teaches a total integration of man's natural and supernatural life, "in an orderly development of his instincts and inclinations, his rich qualities and varied reactions."

The Pope speaks about "man as he is in the sight of God, his creator and Redeemer, as he is in his concrete and his historical reality. ... True religion and profound humaneness are not rivals, they are sisters." He speaks of the majestic unity of life and of an "exalted kindliness," when he couples the Christian life with "a genuine humane humanitarianism."

Keeping religion from economic and political needs and duties is alien to the thinking of the Church: "The Church cannot cut herself off, inert in the privacy of her churches, and thus desert her divinely providential mission of forming the complete man, and thereby collaborating without rest in the construction of the solid foundations of society."

# B. Selected Encyclicals and Addresses of His Holiness Pope Pius XII

*Summi Pontificatus* —
**October 20, 1939**
*On the Function of the State in the Modern world* called for unity in opposing world evils and denounced the errors of "racism and totalitarianism."

*Sertum Laetitiae* —
**November 1, 1939**
*To the Church in the United States* praised the progress of the Church in America and urged Catholics to adhere more strictly to Catholic life and principles.

*Mystici Corporis Christi* —
**June 29, 1943**
*The Mystical Body of Christ* attacked National Socialism: "The Church of God is despised and hated by those who shut their eyes to the light of Christian wisdom and miserably return to the teachings, customs and practices of ancient paganism."

*Divino Afflante Spiritu* —
**September 30, 1943**
*Inspired by the Divine Spirit* defined the most opportune way to promote Biblical studies.

*Papal Directives for the Woman of Today* —
**September 11, 1947**
*Allocution of Pope Pius XII* addressing the Congress of the International Union of Catholic Women's Leagues, Rome, Italy: "Women

must safeguard the rights of the family and participate in the social and political life of the world."

*Fulgens Radiatur* —
**March 21, 1947**
*Fulgens Radiatur* expressed the need for the restoration of the Abbey of Montecassino, destroyed in World War II, to serve as a symbol of faith in an unstable world.

*Mediator Dei* —
**November 20, 1947**
*On Sacred Liturgy* attempted to secure and to inculcate all that is good in the liturgical movement and to delete the unsound principles and practices.

*Humani Generis* —
**August 12, 1950**
*Humani Generis* warned against minimizing the importance of dogma in an attempt to make Catholic teaching more acceptable to non-Catholics. It concerned some false opinions which threatened to undermine the foundations of Catholic Doctrine.

*Menti Nostrae* —
**September 23, 1950**
*Apostolic Exhortation* to the clergy of the entire world on the development of holiness in Priestly Life.

*Munificentissimus Deus* —
**November 1, 1950**
*On the Dogma of the Assumption* that Mary, the Virgin Mother of God, was assumed, body and soul, into the glory of heaven.

*Evangelii Praecones* —
**June 2, 1951**
*On promoting Catholic Missions* "that the word of the Lord may run its course triumphantly," on the occasion of the 25th anniversary of the Encyclical Letter *Rerum Ecclesiae.*

*Moral Questions Affecting Married Life —*
**October 29, 1951 and November 26, 1951**
*Addresses* given to the Italian Catholic Union of Midwives and to the National Congress of the Family Front.

*Fulgens Corona —*
**September 8, 1953**
*On the Marian Year* and on the centenary of the definition of the Dogma of the Immaculate Conception.

*Sacra Virginitas —*
**March 25, 1954**
*On Holy Virginity* confirms the sublimity of the celibate state and the error of advocation of marriage as a higher state.

*Ad Caeli Reginam —*
**October 11, 1954**
*On the Queenship of Mary* states that Mary reigns with her maternal heart over the entire world, just as she is crowned with the diadem of royal glory in heavenly blessedness.

*Haurietis Aquas*
**May 15, 1956**
*On Devotion to the Sacred Heart* begins with the words of the Prophet Isaias: "You shall draw waters with joy out of the Savior's fountains."

*Miranda Prorsus —*
**September 8, 1957**
*On the moral questions* involved in Radio, TV and Motion Pictures.

*Guiding Principles of the Lay Apostolate —*
**October 5, 1957**
**Pope Pius XII** addressed the Second World Congress of the Lay Apostolate: "Christ's Church has no intention of yielding ground to her avowed enemy, atheistic communism, without a struggle. This battle will be fought to the end, but with the weapons of Christ!"

139

*The States of Perfection* —
**December 12, 1957**
**On the States of Perfection** was addressed to the Second General
Congress, which tightened the bonds uniting organizations among
themselves and with the Holy See.

*Applied Psychology* —
**April 10, 1958**
**On Psychotherapy and Religion** was addressed to the Fifth Interna-
tional Congress on Psychotherapy and Clinical Psychology.

*Sacred Music and the Sacred Liturgy* —
**September 3, 1958**
**Instructions of the Sacred Congregation of Rites** were approved by
Pius XII.

# Part XII: Ten Commandments for Peace

*1. Peace is always in God; God is Peace.*

*2. Only men who bow their heads before God are capable of giving the world a true, just and lasting peace.*

*3. Unite, all honest people, to bring closer the victory of human brotherhood and with it the recovery of the world.*

*4. Banish lies and rancor and in their stead let truth and charity reign supreme.*

*5. Affirm human dignity and the orderliness of liberty in living.*

*6. Give generously of aid and relief—State to State, people to people, above and beyond all national boundaries.*

*7. Assure the right of life and independence to all nations, large and small, powerful and weak.*

*8. Work together toward a profound reintegration of that supreme justice which reposes in the dominion of God and is preserved from every human caprice.*

*9. The Church established by God as the rock of human brotherhood and peace can never come to terms with the idol-worshippers of brutal violence.*

*10. Be prepared to make sacrifices to achieve peace.*

*Pius pp. XII*